RBJ aboard *USS Chicago*

A Newsman Remembered
Ralph Burdette Jordan and His Times
1896-1953

by

Robert Smith Jordan

iUniverse, Inc.
Bloomington

A Newsman Remembered
Ralph Burdette Jordan and His Times 1896-1953

iUniverse books may be ordered through booksellers or by contacting:

iUniverse
1663 Liberty Drive
Bloomington, IN 47403
www.iuniverse.com
1-800-Authors (1-800-288-4677)

ISBN: 978-1-4502-8952-8 (pbk)
ISBN: 978-1-4502-8956-6 (cloth)
ISBN: 978-1-4502-8957-3 (ebk)

Printed in the United States of America

iUniverse rev. date: 06/06/2011

To Those Three Generations Who Bear the Name

Ralph Burdette Jordan

and their Progeny

CONTENTS

Acknowledgments

This book had its origins in 1993, when I suffered a heart attack, followed by open-heart double-bypass surgery in Northern Virginia. The calamity occurred on the occasion of a reunion honoring the descendants of Ralph and Mary Jordan, at which every one of their five children were represented – my sister Mary Ellen and I being the last remaining two of the five living. Over the ensuring years, many persons have moved in and out of this project, the most recent being my nephew, Ralph B. "Jock" Jordan III. Bearing the name of his father and grandfather, he was moved to suggest that this unpublished manuscript become a companion to my own published life - *A Diasporan Mormon's Life: Essays of Remembrance*. This I am happy to do because in this way three generations are linked, and I am the last surviving member of my (the second) generation.

My wife Jane stands first, having encouraged me consistently over nearly two decades to engage in family-related research (along with my own professional life as a research professor). Others who deserve mention for one reason or another are: Roger Axtell, Becky Clarke, Jane Hatch Jordan Evert, Jay Gatlin, Claudia Jordan Gibb, Mary Ellen Jordan Haight, Charles M. Hatch, Paul Jordan, Sara Jordan, Maxwell Lawver, Susan Hatch Rasmussen, Kathleen Jordan Seely, William B. Smart, Gibbs M. Smith, Parry Sorensen, Marilyn Hewlett Smoot.

Janesville, Wisconsin, 2010

Foreword

Introduction

Robert Smith Jordan has written extensively and successfully on international relations. He has chosen here to devote his research and analytical skills to his father, Ralph Burdette Jordan. No doubt it is good for the soul of a son to appreciate his father, but sentiment is kept well below the surface here. The story of RBJ had to be written for other reasons.

Exceptional Times

It does not require Bob's extraordinary depth in political history to appreciate that RBJ's life spanned a time unlike any other. RBJ was born in1896. At the time, Joseph Pulitzer's *New York World* and William Randolph Hearst's *New York Journal* were in a circulation battle. Although both were accused of "yellow journalism," there was, in fact, much to write about. The American economy was booming and per capita income was rising. It produced industrialists and financiers such as John D. Rockefeller, Andrew W. Mellon, Andrew Carnegie, J.P. Morgan, and Cornelius Vanderbilt. It also produced the deep depression that followed the Panic of 1893, labor unions, and a demand for social reform. It was, as Mark Twain dubbed it, the Gilded Age.

By the time RBJ died in 1953, the events of his lifetime included the Spanish-American War, the assassination of President McKinley, flight at Kitty Hawk, the Model T, the Panama Canal, income taxes, an influenza pandemic that killed over 50 million people, World War I, Prohibition, Al Capone, Hollywood, the Great Depression, the New Deal, *Gone with the Wind*, and World War II.

These events are the context of RBJ's life, but Bob does not recount them. He takes our historical and social awareness for granted. RBJ was both a newsman searching out and reporting current events; and, at the same time, living in the wake and consequences of those events. Bob's story embraces both of these perspectives. He adds a third perspective to his father's life, identifying him among the then-new generation of middle class aspirants who left their fathers' agrarian dream for higher station. Although it would seem that two world wars and the Great Depression might defeat such aspirations, RBJ succeeded beyond his own dreams.

Family History

For those seeking a broader view of RBJ's generation, Bob has written a private memoir entitled *Two Pioneer Traditions, A Family Memoir*. It includes a brief recital of RBJ's progenitors. Borrowing from it here will set the stage for *A Newsman Remembered*.

Maternal Line

RBJ's parents are Harrison James Jordan and Myrtle Estelle Hanger. RBJ's earliest known American pioneer forebear on his mother's side was Johann Melchior Hengerer. He married Maria Elizabeth in 1723. They were from villages in the Neckar Valley near Heidelberg. They arrived in Philadelphia in 1740. Attracted by affordable prices, their sons, Johann Frederich and Peter, purchased land in Greenbrier County, Woodstock, and Augusta County, Virginia. They moved to Virginia, but retained their close German ties and religious devotion. Johann Frederich died in Augusta in 1799, leaving his wife and thirteen children, among them Carl Hangerer.

By the early 1800's, Carl had Anglicized his given name to Charles and the family name to Hanger. He and his wife, Susannah, migrated west to Ohio, the direction in which many German settlers were moving at the time, along with the national trend.

RBJ's great-grandfather, Charles Hanger, Jr., was born in Ohio in 1818. He was still in Ohio when he married Sarah Jane Burgess in 1844, and when their son, Frederick Allen, was born. Frederick Allen became a butcher and married Eudorah Kirkpatrick in 1873. They had five children, including RBJ's mother, Myrtle Estelle, who was born April 8, 1875.

Paternal Line

Less is known of RBJ's father's side. RBJ's grandfather is John Harris Jordan, born in 1834 in Ohio. In 1857, he married Mary Ellen Browning, who was born in1845 in Des Moines, Iowa. They had a daughter, Lavicia A., and two sons, F. Burdette and Harrison "Harry" James.

The youngest, Harry, is RBJ's father. He was born April 5, 1870 in Genesco, Illinois. Harry married Myrtle Estelle Hanger September 22, 1895. RBJ was born to the couple on October 13, 1896 in Des Moines. He was their only child. The source of the name "Ralph" is unknown, but the middle name comes from RBJ's uncle Burdette.

Harry and Myrtle moved to Colorado for work and better air, and then on to Salt Lake City where Harry worked as a printer, among other jobs. *A Newsman Remembered* picks up the story from there.

RBJ's Namesakes

My father is Ralph Burdette Jordan, Jr. He was born August 2, 1922 in Los Angeles. He was the first of five children born to RBJ and Mary Wright Smith. They called him Burdette.

Burdette loved and respected his father, and Bob tells me there was a growing paternal regard for Burdette as he completed college, served in the military, and returned to finish law school. Burdette did not speak of RBJ often, at least during those times I was listening, but he did impress upon me that RBJ was a man's man, and RBJ respected other men of the same sort. I assumed it was the personality of all men of my grandfather's generation. They were all supposed to be durable, resilient, fearless, intelligent, uncomplicated, and independent - cowboys in Buicks. My father strove for that. He added education to the profile. He was worthy of his father's name, and more, as I think a father would want it to be.

Burdette had personality and he enjoyed engaging with people. He was, I imagine, his father's son in that respect. He wanted to be in the know. He read the Bakersfield Californian, the Los Angeles Times, the Daily Journal (a legal newspaper), and the Wall Street Journal daily. He was not particularly deep in any subject, but he was broad—something about everything. Burdette connected with everyone at some level. He was a conversationalist. He quickly found a common interest or experience and away he went. He did not avoid religion or politics. If he found a willing foil, he enjoyed the banter and debate. Wit and humor kept it interesting and light.

Sometimes people connect in quiet, subtle ways. Burdette made those connections too. He understood adversity and disappointment. He gave the sympathetic ear, had the silent exchanges, and was the shoulder they leaned on. He quietly put presents under someone else's Christmas tree, paid another's legal expenses, helped the widow, found the man a job, talked to someone who knew someone who could help, and bought the bishop a new suit.

Burdette married my mother, Kathleen Patricia Jones on 7 June 1948. As big a personality as Burdette was, he was better with Pat. She was everything his equal, but they were not alike. He was noisy; she was quiet. He was intellectual; she was sentimental. He was opinionated; she reserved judgment. His patience ran thin, hers deep. But when she smiled, she had him. She was irresistible. And he needed her. He always looked for her. I often saw their eyes talking across a room, connecting, sharing, reassuring. She straightened his tie and smoothed his collar as he went out in the morning, and unwound him when he came home in the evening.

While RBJ and I never met, I knew his wife, Mary. She was "Nana." She died in 1980, so I had 27 years with her as my widowed grandmother. Her story is not at the forefront of *A Newsman Remembered*, but Bob makes it clear that the dreams of RBJ for his children were accomplished by Mary. She was the one in the trenches.

Our Debt to Bob and Jane

RBJ passed out of the world in September, 1953 at age 57. I arrived six weeks later. My connection with RBJ would be by name only, were it not for the collection and sharing of family history and genealogy by Bob and his wife, Jane. Bob is the consummate political and social observer, researcher, interpreter, and author. Jane is the tireless seeker and recorder of the family lines. Without them, I would have only a vague impression of my grandfather. He would be a shadow in the background of generations closer to me. The work of Bob and Jane perpetuates the assembled facts of his life and allows me to imagine a boy, a young man, a husband, a father, and a grandfather with some degree of accuracy. They have given me another relationship, which are life's most meaningful elements. *A Newsman Remembered* is a gift to his posterity, for which we are very grateful.

Ralph Burdette Jordan III
Visalia, California
December 2010

RBJ, Sr. RBJ, Jr.

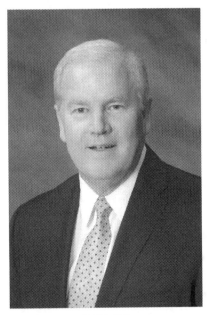

RBJ, III

Chapter One

EARLY CAREER AND MARRIAGE: 1914-1928

"..perfectly ordered families belong to the world of...myth.
The realities of family life are always more diverse, more chaotic..."[1]

Introduction

Standing astride the bridge of the USS *Chicago* in the Coral Sea in May 1942, Ralph (identified henceforth as "RBJ") must have felt that his "time" had arrived. Here he was, in the thick of the greatest naval war in history, being given the opportunity - and the responsibility - of reporting on that war to a world-wide audience through the wires of International News Service (INS). All of his previous years building a newsman's career that spanned delivering papers as a 'teen-ager in Salt Lake City - coming from the "wrong side of the tracks" - through covering the most famous news stories of his generation, must have seemed mere prologue. Along the way to this moment, he had "scooped" the greatest peacetime naval disaster of the time, been instrumental in publicizing and protecting from legal prosecution the most famous actress\evangelist of her time, and nurtured the careers of the movie actors and actresses of Metro-Goldwyn-Mayer (MGM), the most famous motion picture studio of its time. For him, indeed, the past was prologue. How did it all begin?

Early Years

Ralph Burdette Jordan's parents were Myrtle Estelle Hanger, who was born in Clinton, Illinois on April 8, 1875, and Harrison ("Harry") James Jordan, who was born in Genesee, Henry County, Illinois, on April 5, 1870. Myrtle was one of five children born to Frederick Allen Hanger and Eudora Kirkpatrick. Harry was the youngest of three children born to John Harris Jordan and Mary Ellen Browning.[2] He and Myrtle were married in Chicago on September 22, 1895. A picture of her with a harp has written on the back, "best-looking girl at the Chicago Fair." They lived initially in Chicago, but moved to an isolated cabin in Lakeland, Colorado, near Colorado Springs, when he was threatened with tuberculosis. When Myrtle became pregnant, she returned to Des Moines, Iowa, and the home of her in-laws. Harry, according to RBJ's wife Mary, had worked for the local traction company and played professional-grade baseball in Des Moines before his marriage.[3] RBJ was born there on October 13, 1896. When he was twenty-two months old, the young family moved to Salt Lake City, Utah, to ease Harry's persistent lung condition.[4] Harry entered the lithography business with a friend from boyhood, Earl Russell.

RBJ's birth certificate showed him as "unnamed." In fact his name was Ralph Burdette Jordan, after his uncle Burdette Jordan. This inaugurated the three-generation lineage of persons with this name, and which is the inspiration for this book. While RBJ was growing up, the family lived on the west side of Salt Lake. The property is now a parking lot for the Hilton Hotel.

RBJ 1906-1912

Little is known of his early childhood in Salt Lake City, but RBJ was a popular student and an all-around athlete at West High School (the old Salt Lake High); its teams were known as the Panthers. He played tackle and half-back, ran the half-mile relay and the 140-yard dash, and was on the baseball team. There, and in college, he was called "Jock" - doubtless because of his athletic prowess. For example, in the 1915-1916 school years, the Panthers were tri-state champions (Utah, Idaho, and Nevada). RBJ weighed about 170 pounds in those days, and stood over six feet tall, with broad shoulders, a thick torso, and slim hips and legs. He had blue eyes, a ruddy complexion, and thick, curly hair, probably reddish-blonde, and a reddish beard. Although he tried to stay in good physical condition, his lifelong tendency to gain weight caused him at various times in his career to be described as "porky" or "chubby". He liked to exercise regularly; his favorite clubs were the Jonathan and the Los Angeles Athletic Clubs, in Los Angeles, where he played squash, and the Pacific Club in Honolulu. While he lived in Salt Lake City, he swam frequently at the Wasatch Plunge. For family recreation, they belonged to the Deauville Beach Club in Santa Monica during the 1930s, and the Westport Beach Club in Playa del Rey in the 1940s.

Moreover, he was president of his senior class, president of the chemistry club, a member of the glee club and the debate team, on the editorial staff of the school newspaper, the *Red and Black*, and participated in dramatics. Anticipating his future career, he already was writing sports articles for various papers. In fact, as early as 1912, at the age of sixteen, he was writing for *The Telegram Hustler,* the organ of the United Telegram Carriers Association. Its September 15, 1912 issue carried a bylined story by RBJ: *"Joy on a Hayrack: Watermelon Busts Seen From the Roughest Wagon."*[5] He obviously was very much what one might call an "activity boy"! His daughter Mary Ellen inherited some of RBJ's physical traits and many of his talents. She and his son Bob both inherited his blue eyes, his love of writing, and an abiding interest in public and international affairs. .

RBJ continued in athletics at the University of Utah, where he played freshman football and reported on sports activities. When the United States entered the war in Europe in 1917, his National Guard unit was called up, interrupting his academic and sports activities. As a private, he was first sent to Fort Douglas in Salt Lake City, then to Camp Grant, Illinois, and later, after training at Camp Hancock, Georgia, he became a machine gun corps officer. He was commissioned on November 25th a lieutenant in the Officer Reserve Corps; not long thereafter he was demobilized as a lieutenant in the infantry.

Myrtle Estelle Hanger Jordan   Harrison James Jordan

RBJ's first newspaper story

RBJ in Army fatigues, 1918

Upon returning from the Army in February 1919, RBJ became editor and manager of the *Bingham Press-Bulletin*, having been a reporter for the *Bingham Herald* before the war. The town of Bingham, southeast of Salt Lake City, was the site of the largest open-pit copper mine in the world, and had prospered as a result of the war. With his father, RBJ also ran a job-printing plant in Bingham, and managed two cafes with another partner. One may think it fair to describe him as possessing an aggressively entrepreneurial personality. He was even elected secretary of the Chamber of Commerce!

Even though he received offers from the athletic associations of the University of Chicago and Georgia Tech, RBJ decided to accept the invitation of the popular football coach, E. L. "Dick" Romney to play football for Utah State, or the "A.C." as it was then called.[6] A Bingham newspaper article about RBJ's going to Logan, described him as "...a congenial, jovial, companionable fellow, one whom men admire and ladies adore." Another paper on the same subject commented: "He is well known in athletic circles as one of the best football players in the state and he will be one of the strong men with the Aggies next season."[7] Much later, RBJ described how he first met Romney:

> This is the expose', the unmasking, of Dick Romney, director of athletics at Utah State, one of the country's noted coaches. But first, let's appraise him properly: lead off with the good. At the old Salt Lake High School, before there were any East Highs, South Highs, etc.; at that old collection of buildings, where a new West High now stands, and on an athletic field strewn not with soft, green grass, but with hard, gray rocks, a boy wrote athletic history who had very little except determination at the start. But he had plenty of what is politely called courage, to go with his determination, and the combination

led to some interesting and amazing results..... Well, much to our surprise, he went out for Freshman football at the University, and more to our surprise, he wound up first-string fullback, although I always expected to see him jump in the hip-pocket of one of the big boys who ran on either side of him....All-conference back, All-American forward, conference hundred and four-forty champ, and a great man behind the plate.... He certainly was suffering from an acute attack of carelessness when he painted a glowing picture of Logan's halls of learning to me; when he instilled in me such a burning desire to drink from the fountains of knowledge and logic that could be found only in the little city in the great valley of the Cache, that I raced breathlessly to that storied goal and called for a pair of moleskins [football pants].[8]

RBJ also recalled an early experience after arriving in Logan:

Dropping off a train at Logan..., I was greeted by Dick Romney, the Utah State coach, who said, "Welcome, this is a grand place. It's nice to see you; there's something I wish you'd do." One thing about Dick - he always was full of ideas. This idea led to several near-riots. I was to meet a later train and welcome another football prospect, one James E. McDonald, from Whitehall, Montana....Like most of us at that time, he'd just been discharged from the army, and leaped to the station platform like a gazelle, if there are any 220-pound gazelles about 3 feet 4 inches in height, with his piano legs encased in wrapped leggings and the rest of him draped in half civilian, half uniform garb,

> an ensemble set off with some distinction by a
> big cowboy hat. "Glad to meetcha; when do we
> eat?" said Frog [i.e. McDonald]. Following Dick's
> instructions, I marched him, via a restaurant, to
> a neat little three-room apartment in the home of
> Mrs. Haight - a patient, kind woman - near the
> street car line which ran from the depot to the
> college, and introduced him to the other occupants
> of the suite, Glen Dee and Louis Falk, a couple of
> capable backs who'd been romping around army
> gridirons for a semester or so.[9]

As fate would have it, it was at the A.C. that RBJ met Mary
Wright Smith, daughter of Orson Guerney and Mary Ellen
Wright Smith.[10] Although a Methodist by upbringing, RBJ
married into the Mormon culture, and later was baptized into the
Mormon Church. But, like so many of his Utah- and Mormon-
bred contemporaries, he was more interested in adapting to the
"popular culture" that was evolving elsewhere, particularly in
California, than committing himself to the then largely still rural
and small-town Mormon culture of the Intermountain West.

Their Courtship

Mary Wright Smith, after graduating from high school, was also at
the A.C. She was a part-time student of business and a secretary in
the office of E. G. Peterson, President of the A.C. since 1916; at least
part of her time in the President's office was spent directly under
the supervision of Wilford C. Brimley, who was "Secretary to the
President" from 1918 to 1920.[11] It was doubtless at "Old Main," the
administration building, where RBJ and Mary met.[12] RBJ was later
to describe "Old Main" as "... the fine old building in which the
school was founded, mellow and dignified, now being surrounded
with many later structures."[13] When he was established in his career,
RBJ returned to the campus and, speaking at convocation, shared
his impression of President Peterson: "It was a genuine pleasure

to talk with this man, for he had personality, he was keenly alive to the problems of his time. He was stimulating, the best type of American college executive, a fine influence for his students and his community."[14]

RBJ and Mary both were known as being fun-loving, and neither appeared to be too much involved in the serious academic side of college life. "Mary was lots of fun. She was dainty. She only weighed 108 pounds. She was witty and had a keen mind."[15] Mary was indeed a pert young lady with a ready smile. Referring to their mother, her sister Olena went even further: "She had a wonderful sense of humor and made others happy. Her daughter Mary is so like her in this respect."[16] As events were to reveal, Mary also had a mind of her own.

The crisis in their courtship came when RBJ was offered a football scholarship at St. Mary's College in far-away Northern California. In those days, St. Mary's was becoming a football powerhouse under Coach Edward P. "Slip" Madigan, who had played for Notre Dame.[17] But before RBJ succumbed to Madigan's recruiting blandishments, apparently he had already accepted a newly-created position in the athletic department at the "U" and was living in Salt Lake City: "[The] first step to rehabilitate athletics at the University of Utah was taken by the athletic council when it appointed Ralph Jordan, a Salt Lake newspaper man, as athletic manager on the east bench. He will direct all athletics from a business viewpoint, and will be given almost unlimited power in putting all branches of sports before the public, so far as the University of Utah is concerned...."[18] He was also at the time automobile editor of the *Salt Lake Tribune*. The story is told that he drove to Logan to see Mary in a "spiffy" Auburn Beauty Six, but the effect was ruined when the top blew off. During his short tenure at the "U," he took some law courses, and for the rest of his life regretted not having studied law and completing his formal education.[19]

Already a career pattern was emerging. It started with the development of his obviously outstanding athletic abilities and the reporting of sports events which created a state-wide reputation. The next step was that of managing sports activities and reporting and editing on a broader scene. Finally, he embarked on a full-time career in journalism, public relations, war reporting, and motion picture publicity.

RBJ apparently knew how to combine an impressive physical presence with an energetic and winning personality. He suffered, however, from having too many opportunities arise simultaneously. He seemed to be always trying to keep his options open, seizing the career opportunity that appeared most promising to him at the moment, and not considering carefully what the future might bring. Prudence and caution were not his hallmarks, nor are they, for that matter, of any "crack" reporter. Understandably, he apparently did not find it difficult to forsake the opportunity at the "U" in order to go to California.

Mary decided that if she let him go off alone, she would lose him. In her history, Mary says that she happened to be in Salt Lake City at the time. Although she claimed that her dating RBJ did not create tensions in the family, her brother George says otherwise: "She met this Ralph Jordan and they seemed to like each other much to the dislike of my father Orson Smith, Ralph not being L.D.S." Their son Bill commented: "Mary was greatly taken with the football players and they were likewise smitten with her. They were frequently seen around the Smith homestead. One of them, Ralph Jordan, was really smitten by her. He was afraid of her father, however. One night he was standing on the street corner smoking (he was not then a Mormon), Father Smith came by and Ralph swallowed his cigarette."[20]

Orson Gurney Smith   Mary Ellen Wright Smith

So they slipped away to Provo to be married on August 12, 1921, by a friend who was the town clerk. They then went to Bingham to tell his parents, who, given the then-prevailing sentiments, might well have not approved of their only son marrying into a polygamous Mormon family. But, since he was twenty-five and she was twenty-three, no one could claim they were too young to marry. They then wired Logan the news, for in those days it was a bold, even defiant, act for a young Mormon girl to marry a non-Mormon. Mary's sister Olena described the situation:

Sid Spencer asked Mary if he could marry Mary. He took her on a trip to Bear Lake with a group from school. Ralph Jordan heard about the trip to Bear Lake and he went there and asked Mary to marry him. She consented to Ralph and went with him to Provo, Utah. They were married by a Justice of the Peace.... Father wouldn't stay home, but Mary did, and I invited all the family available. I told Mary that they would always regret it if they didn't stay and welcome them. In the middle of the dinner Father walked in. He went right through the dining room to the front room. He was hurt. It was August 1921. Ralph sat next to Auntie [Orson's second wife]. She never talked much. He thought that she was mad at him. It was the first time he ever ate carrots. After finishing dinner, Ralph went into the front room to face Father. When the dishes were done, Mary joined them and found them discussing mining in Bingham Canyon.[21]

Another version of the episode had it that there was much anxiety about what Orson Smith would say or do about it, being so dedicated to the Church. When, at Olena's suggestion, Mary and RBJ showed up for the family dinner on the Sunday after their secret marriage, everyone in the family kept their heads down and waited for what they anticipated would be a storm. Instead, after leaving the house, he returned and asked RBJ to come with him to his study, while everyone else waited in the dining room with trepidation. They waited apprehensively for about an hour, fearing the worst. But RBJ and his new father-in-law finally emerged, after Mary had gone to see what was happening. They were smiling and convivial, to everyone's surprise and relief. Apparently they had been discussing mining, and that was that!

In fact, RBJ claimed that he had met Smith earlier, while dating Mary, and had told him that he was living in Bingham Canyon. RBJ made a point of saying that he lived "near the top" of the canyon, and that the higher you went the tougher it got. Apparently Smith was not impressed. Olena recalled the story differently: "Cliff Meyers from Bingham Canyon was Mary's date. Father met him at the door and asked him in. Father started to ask him the usual questions. Mr. Meyers answered them all in one breath, 'I am from Bingham. You know Bingham is one long street, all uphill. The higher the hill, the taller the houses and the tougher the people. I live in the last house on the top of the hill.' Father didn't say another word. He went out of the room and told Mary not to go with him again."[22]

Mary's mother liked RBJ because she came to know him when they were both active in Republican Party affairs in Logan. Her explanation for having chosen to be a Republican is poignant:

"I was asked why a Republican and answered, 'I took four little children clinging to my skirts under a foreign flag in my maiden name and voted for a Republican. They legalized the children, and McKinley was the man elected.'"[23]

It has sometimes been observed that Mary and RBJ's marriage had tensions not shared by her sisters because they married Mormons and she did not. From what is known of the marriages of Mary's brothers and sisters, the quality of their marriages appeared to be no better or worse than Mary's.[24]

Reporting and Editing for the *Los Angeles Examiner*

Mary was not loath to leave behind the particularism of a small Mormon agricultural community, yet she wanted to preserve and transmit to her own family unit the values that the Logan community had inculcated in her, and which fundamentally formed the foundation of her personality. RBJ, like so many of his Utah - and Mormon-bred contemporaries, was more interested in adapting to the "popular culture" that was evolving elsewhere, especially in California; he had little difficulty leaving Utah behind him.

When he left for St. Mary's, Mary hoped to join him soon, but he stayed at St. Mary's less than one season. Instead of finishing college by playing football, he went to Los Angeles to a job as a rewrite man and police reporter for the *Los Angeles Examiner*. As it was put: "... I can remember Ralph saying soon after [going to St. Mary's] I need to take care of my wife."[25] He apparently just looked around and took what seemed promising at the time. His life was taking a turn in a direction for which one may doubt that he had specifically planned, although he had consciously prepared himself for this career "break."

This, then, marked the real beginning of their marriage, one that was to last over thirty years. They lived at first in a little apartment on Grand Avenue, near the *Examiner* building. Since his salary was very modest, Mary supplemented their earnings by working as the night telephone operator at the apartment. RBJ did not know about this because he worked nights as a police reporter. In fact, he wore a gun and was deputized by the sheriff because reporters were often at the scene of the crime before the police. Rookie reporters started out on the hotel beat, and then progressed to police reporting, which meant covering the murders and underworld scandals. When RBJ discovered what she was doing, he insisted that she quit because this was a tough section of Los Angeles, and RBJ knew (and Mary didn't) that the operator that she had replaced had been murdered.[26] In 1922, when Burdette was due, they moved to a rented house near Broadway and 59th Street, where RBJ could take the streetcar to work.[27]

Life for RBJ as a rewrite man in the city room was described thus: "Dark, airless, noisy, and crowded beyond anything you would believe. At right angles was the city desk, copy went from the city editor to the copy desk, built like a crap table with one man in the slot and the rest around the rim. The flow got more frenzied as the deadline of each edition approached every hour or so. Behind the copy desk was the door into the composing room, where ink-stained overalled linotype operators set the copy for the big presses and *they* got more frantic too."[28] He described it: "Once on a big Los Angeles newspaper I was one of a battery of six rewrite men. We took information by telephone from reporters on various 'beats' around the city and whipped it into stories....the phones would jangle, the city editor and his assistants scream in nervous excitement, photographers dash in and out like they were going to a fire, which they probably were, and typewriters bang with machine-gun sharpness while over all the gigantic presses would send up their deep roar from the basement."[29]

While night city editor RBJ got one of the biggest "scoops" of his career. He remembered it in a column in another newspaper many years later:

The story for which your correspondent is best known in the newspaper world, providing he is known at all, developed like this: One night at the city desk of the Los Angeles Examiner the phone rang. The Southern Pacific Railroad's dispatcher at San Luis Obispo, half way between Los Angeles and San Francisco, asked if we knew anything about some ships being wrecked at Point Honda which is near San Luis Obispo. I said no, that it undoubtedly wasn't true or we would have heard it from the many sources of information available to a newspaper. He said a track walker in the employ of the railroad had called him from Point Honda and said some war ships were on the rocks there. We agreed the track walker was having a hallucination. An hour later the dispatcher was on the phone again. His track walker was insistent there were war ships wrecked at Point Honda. This time I had just sense enough - which is very little sense - to check around, and discovered that a squadron of U.S. destroyers had left San Francisco for San Diego for a fast run, had been out long enough to be at Point Honda and that the lighthouse at the point was worried because the squadron's radio had suddenly gone silent, had quit making for radio bearings.

It was about 10 o'clock on a Saturday night by the time I piled a couple of reporters and two photographers into a limousine driven by a noted race driver and started for Point Honda, 200 miles away. Leaving the main coast highway at Lompoc, we swerved down some secondary roads to the coast, and then got stuck in the sand. Not knowing whether to walk north or south along the coast, for

I wasn't sure where we were and there was no place to find out, I flipped a nickel. It came up heads, so we went south, and in only a few miles, just as daylight was breaking, came over a hill and looked down upon the worst disaster in the peacetime history of the United States Navy. Eleven destroyers had crashed onto the shore. Two had pulled off, but the remaining nine were fast aground, one broken in two on a saddle of rocks, one capsized with a gaping hole in her side; all were wrecked.

Officers and men were trying to swim ashore through the heavy surf which was coated thickly with oil. It was a shocking experience and between 20 and 30 sailors drowned. The Southern Pacific tracks were not far from the shore at this point, and from a section shanty and over a railroad phone I called my friend, the dispatcher at San Louis Obispo, and asked him to send me a lineman and a Morse operator, both of which he did pronto. The lineman cut a wire into my office in Los Angeles and the operator sent my story as fast as I could write it. The result was a clean beat. My paper hit the street with an extra containing four pages of story and pictures, early Sunday, while our opposition was just getting around to investigating rumors of a wreck.

However, let's examine the causes of this success, important to me and my newspaper. We first heard about it because the railroad dispatcher happened to be a reader of my paper. If he had been a subscriber to our opposition, they would have received the break and we would have been left floundering. If the nickel had fallen the other way, I and my crew would have gone the wrong direction on the beach and would never have found the scene of the disaster. Just plain luck? Absolutely. You've got to be lucky in this business, and I suspect the same holds true of other businesses.[30]

The *Times* and the *Examiner* were bitter rivals. Norman Chandler, whose family owned the *Times*, was as much a newspaper buccaneer as the *Examiner's* owner, William Randolph Hearst: "For all of Norman Chandler's personal attractiveness he published a paper devoid of fairness and justice....His paper slew his enemies - Democrats, labor unions....The friends of the Chandlers were written about as they wished; their enemies were deprived of space, or attacked."[31]

Because the *Examiner* was a morning newspaper, the night city editor was the main person responsible for "putting to bed" the morning's edition. Any fast-breaking news had to be handled by the night city editor, which required some speedy judgment calls, since the competition among the several newspapers in Los Angeles at that time for the "scoop" was intense.[32]

Another famous story which RBJ covered was the murder of Hollywood producer William Desmond Taylor in 1922. It ruined the career of movie star Mabel Normand, who along with the comedian Roscoe C. "Fatty" Arbuckle, worked for Mack Sennett's Keystone Pictures, doing the famous Keystone Comedies. Normand was innocent, although implicated. As Adela Rogers St. Johns observed: "Let me present in truth the Case of the Hollywood Producer, the Child Star and her Smother-Mother and with it the solution to Hollywood's deepest mystery. As for Mabel, it is true that night after night she'd been at Taylor's apartment. He gave her the man companionship she'd been used to in her work association with Sennett. He was, she told me, her close friend, but they had never spoken a word of love nor exchanged more than a friendly kiss. I believed her because Mabel always told the truth. But to the world it was, of course, a love affair and anything including murder can come of *that*."[33]

In another Hollywood scandal, "Fatty" Arbuckle was accused of murder. Again RBJ was the newsman covering the trials. After the departure of Charlie Chaplin from Keystone, Arbuckle was the top comedian on the lot and therefore a nationally and internationally known celebrity in Mack Sennett comedies. In September 1921 Arbuckle was accused of causing the death of an actress and model named Virginia Rappe, who died after a party at Arbuckle's suite at the St. Francis Hotel. He had reserved the suite for a weekend of relaxation after completing a movie; there was plenty of bootleg liquor - this was during Prohibition - and plenty of comings and goings, and little accountability. Although Rappe died the following day from peritonitis, Arbuckle was accused of what today is called sexual abuse and indicted for manslaughter.[34] After protracted and sensational trials in early 1922, he was acquitted, but not until he had become the first Hollywood star to be blacklisted by the so-called Hays Office of the Motion Pictures Producers and Directors of America.[35] Because of Hollywood's increasing notoriety after World War I due to the well-publicized high living of its stars, producers, directors - indeed, all of those in the world of film-making - pressure had been brought to bear on the industry to "clean up its act." The blacklisting damaged Arbuckle's career almost as much as the trials.

For this memoir, it is noteworthy that as a newsman, RBJ was in the thick of Hollywood's tribulations almost from the time that he had arrived in Los Angeles. Understandably, he was frequently away from home covering a story, or working nights, so Mary could not rely on him domestically. Having been an only child and therefore raised in essentially an adult environment, he probably was never entirely comfortable living in a household full of children and assorted relatives, although perhaps precisely because of this, he "adopted" Mary's large family. In any event, he was undoubtedly very close to his mother, which is why, when she died under mysterious circumstances, he was devastated and could not return to work for several months.

Harry and Myrtle Estelle Jordan had also moved to California from Utah, following RBJ; they lived in an area called Stonehurst, at 4227 Sheldon Avenue, in the San Fernando Valley. The inspiration for the name comes from the rock quarries nearby that must have been the source for the building materials. With some partners, RBJ had invested in Stonehurst in this "roarin' twenties" period of intense real estate speculation, and the subdivision still exists. When the town of Burbank would not authorize light and water connections to Stonehurst - instead saying it was Van Nuys' responsibility - RBJ ran a piece in the *Examiner* "...about this attractive secretary at Burbank in the clerk's office who could not get things right. When they returned to [the clerk's office after the story ran] the secretary said: 'It is certainly strange that your case is like that man's in the paper today.' Ralph said that he wrote that and they should see the next day's he was preparing. They quickly got action."[36]

Harry Jordan worked as a circulation manager or distributor in the Valley for the *Examiner*, a job which RBJ doubtless had obtained for him. Their Stonehurst house was small, but it was surrounded by enough land for the raising of chickens. On the night of July 20, 1926, RBJ's parents heard noises in their chicken coop, and fearing a predator was disturbing their chickens, Myrtle went out to investigate. She was accidentally shot either by herself as she stumbled in the dark or by Harry. There must not have been nearby neighbors to rely on when such exigencies arose, for she died. RBJ had hoped to give the Stonehurst house to his parents as a gift, but he lost possession of it through foreclosure when the subsequent illness prevented him from working for a period of time.

By the time Mary Ellen was born on April 21, 1927, the growing family had moved from an apartment on North Van Ness Avenue near Hollywood Boulevard, to a Spanish-style house at 4237 West 59th Place, near Broadway, not far from the Boyle Heights section of Los Angeles.[37] The area in which they had lived on North Van Ness Avenue was inhabited by many persons connected to the film industry. For example, Mabel Normand lived at Seventh and Figueroa and Adela Rogers St. Johns lived on North Wilton Place. The apartments often were built around a garden square, facing Hollywood Boulevard, or near it, with delivery alleys to the rear.

RBJ, Mary, Fred, Mary Ellen, Burdette, 1928

Utahn Clara Kimball Young movie poster

Along with motion pictures, Southern California was developing a favorable reputation as a retirement community for Midwesterners and as a winter watering hole for wealthy Easterners.[38] The real estate market was booming in the 1920s because: "...between 1920 and 1924 at least one hundred thousand people a year poured into Los Angeles alone....The newcomers were home-seekers...In two years fourteen hundred new tracts were opened in Los Angeles County."[39] A bus travelogue of July 1929 included these items: "On the left you enter Fremont Place... No. 56 is the former home of Mary Pickford....the big house with the palms; they are Hawaiian palms and were brought over here at enormous cost...; The large white school on the corner is the Marlborough School for Girls. Eight years ago this was so far out in the country that they refused to deliver milk there....; this now brings us to the Wilshire Country Club. Memberships in this club cost $5,000. Solicitors became obnoxious during the summer of 1921, trying to sell memberships at $100 each...."[40]

To the dismay of the city fathers, as suggested above, Los Angeles was acquiring a reputation as a freewheeling city where "anything goes". "In a city that contained few monuments or buildings reflecting the nineteenth-century Anglo-Saxon culture, there seemed to be a release from the restraint of tradition.... The vague, mythic term 'Hollywood' connoted a way of life unfolding in the reclusive neighborhoods of Beverly Hills, Santa Monica, and Brentwood. Freed from any nearby reminders of social responsibility, in areas cleansed through vice crusades, the stars could create a new, uplifted life without the inhibitions of the past."[41]

The Mormons of RBJ and Mary's' generation were not immune to this attraction, as the following chapter shows. RBJ and this metropolitan environment were made to order for each other, and Mary was willing to go along for the ride which, as revealed in the next chapter, gets even more exciting.

Chapter Two

EVANGELISTIC FUNDAMENTALISM AND AIMEE SEMPLE MCPHERSON

"Like Barnum, she understood the principle that
'there is no such thing as bad publicity.'"[42]

A Phenomenon of 20th Century America

Aimee Semple McPherson was what Max Weber, the German sociologist, would call a "charismatic" figure and her Foursquare Gospel would today be known as a form of "charismatic" religion. She had the uncanny ability to enthrall those with whom she came in contact, and to elicit strong bonds of loyalty and belief in her as a faith healer, comforter, and spiritual "leader."[43] She also aroused strong suspicions that she was a fraud, duping her ever-growing number of converts. Some of her detractors claimed that she used the considerable revenues from her various enterprises to support a non-religious lifestyle, while other detractors claimed that her motives were love of power and fame. Nonetheless, she was without a doubt one of the most famous and powerful women to appear on the Southern California scene at the time that RBJ's career was getting underway.

It did not matter whether she was credible in a rational sense; her "presence" was what mattered. "Enthusiasts came less to hear Aimee's gospel than to see Aimee. The individual who spoke the words lent them power. 'Let Mrs. McPherson's deliverances be divorced from Mrs. McPherson's personality,' wrote a contemporary, 'and they fall to the depths of the banal....Her influence is incredible....She is today one of the most amazing phenomena of power in this feverish power-insane United States.'"[44] The kind of sensationalist journalism that characterized both of the major Los Angeles newspapers at the time - the *Examiner* and the *Times* - were tailor-made for Aimee Semple McPherson.

How could someone with her attributes achieve such quick success in Southern California at this particular time? Her elevation to such status was partly because of the nature of the times. In the late 1920s and the aftermath of the disaster of World War I, America (and Europe) was in the throes of sharp swings between pessimism about the future of "civilization" and elation about the future of "capitalism," and its ability to bring financial security and the good life to the masses. When capitalism failed in the Depression that began in 1929, there was widespread despair and consequently a search for alternative forms of social as well as religious "salvation." Masses of people were being displaced, joining those who, during the 1920s, were retiring to a climate where their limited pensions would go farther. And so: "She had come, of course, to the right place to launch an evangel of joyousness. In the decade 1920-1930, 1,270,000 new residents swept into the County of Los Angeles, with the peak of this movement being reached in 1923, the year the temple was founded....Migration severs allegiances and weakens old loyalties. It creates the social fluidity out of which new cults grow and flourish. Nine out of ten of Aimee's followers were converts from the orthodox Protestant creeds...aching with loneliness and the feeling of 'wanting to know someone,' they found their heart's desire in Angelus Temple, Sister Aimee, and the Shared Happiness of Kindred Souls."[45]

A large percentage of her followers were elderly, retired people escaping the harsh winters of the Midwest. They had been practicing Baptists, Methodists, and Presbyterians. They were, in large part, the "middle class," self-sufficient, but frugal.[46] Later, they were from all walks of life, and even from what we would today call minority backgrounds. This was the social and economic environment in which Aimee and her Church of the Foursquare Gospel flourished in such a profound way. She offered a message of hope and redemption - emphasizing not the usual evangelical\ fundamentalist message that sinners are to be punished, but rather that sinners and saints alike can be saved.

She did not neglect the unfortunate, but rather reached out to the homeless and destitute. For example, she created a commissary and welfare program that presaged the public welfare programs that came later under the New Deal.[47] As it was described: "She kept tens of thousands of people from starving to death.... When the schools stopped feeding children free lunches, Aimee took over the program. When city welfare agencies staggered under the load of beggars, the women of Angelus Temple sewed quilts and baked loaves of bread by the thousands. When bread lines stretched for city blocks and 'Brother Can You Spare a Dime?' was a hit song, when federal programs and the other charities faltered in a tangle of red tape, Angelus Temple was the only place *anyone* could get a meal, clothing, and blankets, no questions asked. Aimee's policy was 'give first and investigate afterward.' While this led to a certain amount of waste, it also alleviated suffering on an epic scale."[48]

Her followers remained strikingly devoted to "Sister" as she was affectionately called, as she went from one highly-publicized, and often controversial, episode to another. As a tent-revivalist, she was unparalleled, even though as a manager and institution-builder, she had some serious shortcomings. But how many of the American fundamentalist Christian founding "prophets" that emerged during the 19th and early 20th centuries have displayed both entrepreneurial and managerial skills? It was the ceaseless publicity and her growing fame that in part attracted those who became "saved" through her preaching. This devotion gave her a personal audience at Angelus Temple, from which night after night she would stage her famous dramatic sermons, which could be used to promote or discredit whatever idea or persons she chose. But also, she could reach a wider audience from her own radio station, KFSG (Kall Foursquare Gospel). It is thus interesting, if not necessarily significant, that Aimee Semple McPherson, hired RBJ away from the *Los Angeles Examiner* in January 1927 to be her chief press agent, manager, and advisor.

In sum, Aimee Semple McPherson - known only as "Sister" or as "Aimee" - proved to be a genius at self-promotion.[49] "Anything with press on it received quick recognition from Aimee's team. Ralph Jordan and Ralph Wheelwright of the *Los Angeles Examiner* kept her covered all the time because she was in that class as *news* and also, both of them admitted afterwards, they were madly in love with her."[50] Men were "in love" with her the way they were with the reigning movie stars of the period, such as Mary Pickford and Gloria Swanson. She dazzled them. As one observer put it at the time: "More talk about Aimee there was than any other woman in California, not excepting movie stars. Her following is sensational in numbers..."[51] Put another way: "The scandalmongers' effect on journalism in the 1920's is well known. They created a kind of 'inflation' of news interest in personalities, lowering standards of privacy. But reporters who covered Hollywood also covered City Hall, the racetrack, and Angelus Temple. Fast-breaking political news that went out on the wire from Hearst's *Examiner* vied with reports on Paulette Goddard's eyelashes, and [Charlie] Chaplin's latest escapade. Everyone in the public eye, everyone whose business depended upon publicity, was affected."[52]

(1) Aimee Semple McPherson in 1923, three years before her disappearance

Aimee

(8) Sister rising from the waves: a composite picture sold by Ocean Park concessionaires while the search went on

Aimee rising heavenward

Ocean Park;

Tilden Dakin redwoods painting

RBJ's Involvement in her "Disappearance"

This was a crucial turning-point in her career, although it was never made clear in the late spring of 1926 whether Aimee was engaging in self-promotion, or in scandalous behavior, when she "disappeared" while swimming off a pier in Ocean Park on May 18th.[53] RBJ was involved in the case from its beginning: "When Aimee disappeared into the ocean and the whole country was in suspense I went down with Jordan and Ralph Wheelwright to the sands off Ocean Park where she had gone for a swim and never came back. For days, nights, her followers were kneeling in the sands, praying, looking for her to come back walking on the water."[54] She was presumed dead until she reappeared on June 23rd in a remote corner of the Arizona desert near Douglas, not far from the Mexican border. RBJ covered for the *Examiner* the disappearance story and the subsequent high-profile investigation of the circumstances of the "disappearance," including allegations that it was a cover-up for an affair she was carrying on with her radio station engineer, Kenneth G. Ormiston.

"The city seethed with rumors, and so did Angelus Temple. Strange faces were appearing there - outsiders, worldly people, and especially two newspapermen, one until recently with the *Examiner* and the other from the *Times*."[55] "The betting popularly was that Aimee would never come to trial. It was noted, for example: 'In this venture, Aimee had the encouragement of Ralph Jordan, a former reporter for Hearst's *Los Angeles Examiner*. Jordan...had become indispensable to Aimee during the hearings. He had helped her deal with the press, intervening with Hearst on the evangelist's behalf. Aimee preferred Jordan's advice to her own chief counsel's. By January the fast-talking Jordan was on the Angelus Temple payroll as the personal road manager of Aimee's vindication tour."[56]

One author put it this way: "...she had secretly added two more men to her private staff, two reporters who had been active in investigating the scandal against her. They were Ralph

Jordan of the *Examiner* and James Kendrick of the *Times*. One would ghostwrite a book for Aimee explaining her version of the kidnaping. The other would act as her personal manager on a 'vindication tour' to begin as soon as the trial closed. It would cost Aimee incalculable thousands of dollars, but it would work."[57]
By January 1927: "...rumors of a dismissal persisted. Around Angelus Temple reporters caught whispers that Sister was placing her reliance in three 'deliverers' - believed to be her two newspaper consultants and a press agent who had been hired before the preliminary hearing - and there were frightened allusions to 'payoffs.'"[58]

It was alleged that: "... Jordan had gone to William Randolph Hearst, the publisher, and had argued that the continuation of the 'Aimee case' would be bad for the city and on the grounds of the public good should be halted. Hearst, it was said, was inclined to agree. His influence in Los Angeles was potent, and a few days after the reported talk with Jordan, Hearst's *Examiner* did quote [District Attorney] Keyes as saying he intended to dissolve the case."[59] Keyes denied the rumor, but subsequently did dismiss the case just before it would have gone to trial, stating that she could only be judged: "...in the only court of her jurisdiction - the court of public opinion."[60]

That the rumors concerning a Hearst intervention had some substance was the fact that it turned out that she and RBJ:

> ...were maintaining a secret account in a bank far from Angelus Temple [but not far from RBJ's home], in which large deposits had been made and from which large sums had been withdrawn.... This joint account had been at the 39th Street and Western Avenue branch of the Security-First National Bank in the names "Elizabeth and Edith Johnson." Subsequent investigation would indicate that deposits of roughly one hundred thousand dollars had been made, against which checks

for sixteen thousand, fourteen thousand, eight thousand, and similar sums had been cashed. The account, opened in August, 1927, had been closed out in April, 1928. These were about the dates between which Ralph Jordan had been acting as business manager of Angelus Temple. [61]

Thus there was more than a strong presumption that RBJ had been instrumental in dispensing these funds in connection with the dismissal of the case. Whether this was in fact what occurred - and the subsequent efforts of the district attorney and the judge neither proved nor disproved the assumption - Aimee's seizing control over these funds and their disappearance around the time of her trial could give the appearance of being more than coincidental.

Furthermore, RBJ might have helped her in another way financially: "...Sister's pleas to her followers to make up the twenty-five thousand-dollar deficit in her church's finances.... Just previously, Aimee had called her church board together and told them about the notes, saying they had been given to secure a loan from Ralph Jordan that had been needed to tide things over after her mother had left. She said the notes were due. Jordan and his wife had appeared and confirmed the loan, stating that they had mortgaged their home to raise the cash. On the basis of these representations, the board had sanctioned an appeal to the membership for a special contribution."[62]

What is central to this entire episode is the inescapable fact that RBJ was instrumental in her avoiding being discredited through what to many persons was a sexual scandal, coupled with financial mismanagement, if not more. Angelus Temple and the entire Foursquare Gospel enterprise had been put seriously at risk. Her mother Minnie Kennedy certainly thought so, as did her son, Rolf.[63]

Roland Rich Woolley, the attorney who defended her in the court trials following her disappearance and reappearance, was also a Mormon. When he found out that Aimee and her mother Minnie were manipulating events behind his back, and that they were carrying on a very public relations effort to buttress Aimee's case and to discredit any threats to that story - often thereby frustrating the normal legal processes - he resigned. But he was himself caught in these attempts: "....in a new version of her introduction to the plot, Mrs. [Lorraine] Wiseman [who had come forward as the purported other woman - Miss X] accused Roland Rich Woolley of being the principal instigator. She said Woolley drew her into the hoax through his brother, Jack Woolley, who was the mysterious 'Mr. Martin' she met in San Francisco. When she first arrived in Los Angeles, she added, she went directly to Woolley's office, where she got instructions on how to frame the 'Miss X' evidence."[64] After much furor and vigorous denials, which required him to endure a day's questioning by the District Attorney and his staff, at considerable personal expense, he was able to clear himself of any complicity in perpetrating a hoax.[65]

Another of her managers - who succeeded RBJ - was Cromwell Ormsby, who, although not a newspaperman, was equally, if not more controversial within the Foursquare community than had been RBJ. This controversy, among other things, was over the management of Aimee's finances.[66] Interestingly, Ormsby also had Utah origins, having come to California from Logan.[67] As can be seen, the Mormon\Utah connection in regard to Aimee Semple McPherson was very strong.

This observation is not too far off the mark in explaining RBJ's and Ormsby's involvement with Aimee: "In desperation to find someone other than her mother to take charge of business matters, Aimee seems to have agreed, time and again, to surrender her will completely to any man who appeared fit for the job. There were Ralph Jordan and Cromwell Ormsby. Later there would be A.C. Winters and Giles Knight, before [her son] Rolf McPherson finally came to the rescue."[68]

Aimee's ministerial affairs and her financial affairs were intimately intertwined, for she raised large sums of money through her preaching, much of it going to support her welfare activities, but much also going to support her highly dramatized preaching activities. For example, Angelus Temple had been designed and constructed specifically to meet her style of preaching, and it had become a top attraction in Southern California. Her extravagant meetings were very expensive to stage, but they brought in large sums.

Aimee's Impact on the "Theatrics" of Religious Expression

Aimee brought to Los Angeles her own brand of fantasy, just as powerful in its way as the movie maker's fiction. She would prove herself no less inventive than Zukor and Lasky, and as energetic as Goldwyn and Fox - and these giants of the cinema admired her. Angelus Temple had perfect acoustics. In moments of envy certain producers in her audience hoped she might fail so they could take over the Temple and turn it into a theater.

But Aimee had already done that. Her years on the tent-show circuit had taught her that a religious service is sacred drama, a species of nonfictional theater, pure and simple. The problem with denominational churches, said Aimee, was that they had given in to their profane competitors- vaudeville, movies, and 'legitimate theater' - and thereby had lost the attention of their congregations, who took their excitement wherever they could find it....

The Temple was indeed a mixed blessing, a costly haven....She was under pressure to create a religious theater that would guarantee an audience - and she could not repeat herself in her own pulpit... she was a perfect actress....[69]

Mary's sister, Mrs. J. Franklin Woolley, went to one of her services when she was passing through Los Angeles in 1928; she described how Aimee would emerge out of the "bowels" of her Temple. She would come up out of the floor with a mammoth organ playing, dressed in white robes carrying a bouquet of red roses, which was her trademark.[70]

Mary traveled with RBJ on some of his preaching/revival trips for Aimee, although neither one of them were members of Aimee's church, nor were they believers in her ecclesiastical message. On a trip to St. Louis and Chicago, most likely Aimee's "vindication" tour where she preached to large audiences, Mary sold religious literature from a booth. This may have been when Aimee acquired her "Gospel Car," an automobile which gave her flexibility to travel anywhere she wished to preach and convert. She defended her preaching style in the florid language of her autobiography *In the Service of the King*:

> Emotionalism! Kneel just once beside a man's heaving shoulders, beside a woman's shaking form, hear them ask forgiveness in husky broken voices, see their tears fall through their quivering hands to the floor - and then see the joy of a new-born gladness fill their hearts, watch the light of a great happiness leap into their eyes, feel the glow within your own being as they depart with heads erect, faces radiant, know the soul-satisfying gratification of having brought an enduring comfort into the lives of others! Creep into your bed at night, exhausted with the delicious exhaustion that anticipates the efforts of the morrow.[71]

A legacy of one of the promotional ventures in which RBJ was involved remained with the family until Mary's death. Aimee planned a summer camp near Lake Tahoe called Tahoe Cedars, on land specified for this purpose if a tabernacle were built there as well. Then the adjacent lots would be sold off to church members. Unfortunately, the church members - many of whom were trying to weather the financial ravages of the Depression - were not interested in having a summer camp in Northern California while they lived in Southern California. It was reported that: "Ralph Jordan, whom Sister was introducing everywhere as her business manager, was active particularly in the Tahoe Cedars promotion. To launch the expected boom in building lots, Sister announced that she would lead a motorcade of prospective buyers on the four-hundred-mile journey north to dedicate the ground. But when the pilgrimage was made, with Sister bravely leading, only a trickle of followers came behind her."[72] The result was that RBJ came into the possession of five of the lots, which were left undeveloped partly because of zoning restrictions.[73]

Another financially unsuccessful project in which RBJ was involved was the creation of a cemetery so that members of the Foursquare Gospel could be buried next to - or near - the evangelist. It was called Blessed Hope Memorial Park, and a fourteen-acre lot was purchased in Burbank. This project also failed, probably because it became a salesman's extravaganza. In California, since the 1880s, land speculation and real estate promotion had been part and parcel of the state's high-flying way of life. In fairness to Aimee, the notion of "marketing" burial services akin to that of motion pictures, was shared not only by her. Forest Lawn Memorial Park, which was being developed during this time, also introduced many promotional features that in other times and places would have been considered inappropriate for a sacred surrounding.[74] Aimee was, in fact, buried in Forest Lawn.[75]

Somehow, not necessarily connected to Aimee but rather to RBJ's brief foray into running his own public relations business, RBJ came into the possession of two California landscape paintings by Tilden Dakin, who was popular at the time. After Mary's death, the smaller one of a glorious California sunset passed to Mary Ellen, and the larger one of the California redwoods passed to Bob. Mary Ellen, with her son Jim, added other of Dakin's painting to their homes, as did Bob along with his son Bob. In total, there are about fifteen in the possession of the family. Thus it is fair to say that these paintings represent a permanent legacy from the Aimee period of hucksterism to the Jordan family.

During these years since their marriage, it would be almost an understatement to say the RBJ's and Mary's lives had been anything but uneventful! For Mary, with a highly religious, small-town rural background, these years could not help but have confronted her with moral as well as professional dilemmas concerning the course that RBJ's career was taking. National notoriety was not what she had bargained for when she went off to Provo to be married. But it was not at all out of character for an energetic, ambitious man like RBJ to view his horizons as being the beckoning possibilities of California and the Pacific region, which in the "Roaring '20s" was full of color and movement - and above all - opportunity.

Even Governor Henry H. Blood of Utah, in 1939, acknowledged the attraction that the "golden state" of California had to Utahns: "It has often been observed that Utah, geographically and commercially, faces towards the Pacific. Utah looks westward; she trades with the Pacific states, and particularly with California.... During the last quarter century, at least one hundred thousand members of the Mormon Church have migrated to California and have established their homes, their business enterprises and the professions among the friendly people of this state."[76]

From this combination of professional turmoil and expanding domestic responsibilities, RBJ managed to emerge virtually unscathed, thanks (perhaps once again) to the intervention of William Randolph Hearst.

Chapter Three

INTERNATIONAL NEWS SERVICE AND METRO-GOLDWYN-MAYER 1930-1941

"Get It First, But First Get It Right"
"More Stars Than There Are in the Heavens"[77]

Reporting and Administering for
International News Service (INS)

Within a year of the birth of the twins (Bob and Bill) - on June 11, 1929 - the family moved to Oakland. RBJ had returned to the employment of William Randolph Hearst, this time in the San Francisco office of International News Service (INS). Obviously, RBJ's relationship to Aimee Semple McPherson, which had brought him directly to Hearst's attention, did not hinder his career with the Hearst organization, either at this time or later. The press announcement of his subsequent promotion to Pacific Coast Division Manager, issued from the INS headquarters in New York, was quite laudatory:

> The appointment of Ralph B. Jordan as Pacific Coast division news manager of International News Service was announced here today at the

headquarters of the organization....For the past year Jordan has been directing the San Francisco bureau of International News Service. Previously he had been the International News Service star staff writer on the coast, attached to the San Francisco bureau. The new coast news chief came to International News Service six years ago with a record as a reporter and editor which already had established him as 'tops' in the West, particularly along the shores of the Pacific... [When] Jordan came to the coast ...[he] at once stepped into the select class of star reporters, alternating covering the coast's biggest news assignments with directing a big staff as city editor in Los Angeles. He has scored many notable 'beats' and covered and written such famous stories as the William Desmond Taylor murder, the 'Fatty' Arbuckle case, the Point Honda destroyer wreck, the David Lemson case, the San Jose kidnaping and lynchings, the Will Rogers-Wiley Post crash, the Aimee Semple McPherson mystery, and the United States fleet on spectacular maneuvers in the south seas.[78]

INS was founded in 1909 as part of Hearst's journalistic empire, to transmit news via a single Morse telegraph wire, but it was completely independent of the other Hearst properties. It had had a somewhat checkered career since its founding, mostly because in World War I it tended to reflect Hearst's pro-German sentiments. He was intensely patriotic, pro-Irish, and hence, anti-British. The consequence was: "The Hearst anti-British line, including his warm defense of Sir Roger Casement, the Irish patriot executed for holding secret parleys with the Germans, did not go unnoticed in England....On October 11, 1916, the British government retaliated with a stringent and unwarranted measure. It banned the Hearst press from the use of its cables and mails.

The French government followed suit on October 29, while on November 8, the Hearst papers were banned in Canada."[79] INS, dependent on the cable, suffered the same fate, and was also tarnished with the same brush.

However, with the entry of the United States into World War II, Hearst threw himself wholeheartedly onto the side of the Allies, much to the relief of the British.[80] In any event. by the time RBJ had joined the organization, the day-to-day management had largely passed out of Hearst's hands. As part of a massive restructuring of the Hearst properties in August 1927, Universal Service - another news organization - was merged with INS and placed under the direction of Joseph V. Connolly. Connolly, who was to play a pivotal role in RBJ's career, was part of a small group of executives called the "Young Turks," who had been formed under the leadership of Clarence John Shearn to place the Hearst interests on a sound financial as well as managerial basis.[81] By the mid-1930s, INS had about 5,000 correspondents, served approximately 600 newspapers in the United States, and had an annual outlay of $2,500,000.

These efforts continued throughout the 1930s. and indeed until Hearst's death. Fortunately, one beneficial result was that INS was able to compete both in reputation and effectiveness with the other two major American news services of the time - Associated Press and United Press. The Pacific Coast Division News Manager position was increasing in importance because by the late 1920s and the 1930s, California was not only the production center for the motion picture industry, but also for several major oil companies, for trade, commerce and banking. The position was also important because, by then, Hearst conducted his affairs from his various residences in California. The Hearst Building, where INS was located and to which RBJ commuted across the Bay from Oakland, also housed the *San Francisco Examiner* ("The Monarch of the Dailies"). Furthermore, Hearst was intimately involved in the political as well as the commercial life of California - and especially in the movie industry.

While RBJ was working for INS, the staff was guided by a "code of conduct." These "editorial orders" were:

> The only policy of International News Service is absolute impartiality. International News Service must never jump the gun. The facts in every I.N.S. story must be checked personally by the man handling the story. It is a flat order that both sides be told in any story involving controversy or difference of opinion. Editors must be on the alert to prevent any agents or organizations from using the service for propaganda. There is no excuse for sloppy copy-reading. We should have four or five excellent human interest stories from each bureau every day. International News Service is a strictly non-partisan news agency. We want to cover all the news, but make sure that any political matter that is carried is subjected to a close scrutiny. Apply the acid test of, "is it news" to every item. Keep all wires flexible so that the best story available at any given time can move without delay. Stories requested by clients should be moved as promptly as possible. No story is worth a libel suit. Confine your stories to the facts as they develop. "GET IT FIRST, BUT FIRST GET IT RIGHT."[82]

But Hearst was not reluctant to publish private scandal as well as "hard news," and as has been shown, RBJ's career had thrived on both types of journalism. Hearst was not apologetic about this duality:

> I have been asked if there is any justification in publishing news of a private scandal. None whatsoever if it is private and if it is scandal. But news about the actions of private persons ceases to be private when it gets into the public courts. I

once sat next to a man in Washington at a dinner and he kept annoying me by complaining that some one of my newspapers had printed items about his brother's divorce. Finally I told him that it was deplorable and that I would make a compact with him. If he would keep his brother out of the divorce courts I would keep him out of my newspapers, because so far as I know his brother had no other claim to newspaper attention. A good many people who object to the attention newspapers give their private affairs forget that their affairs have become of public interest and public importance through their own fault entirely and through no fault of the newspapers. *A newspaper's right and duty are to print public facts in which the public is interested, whether the individuals concerned are public or private.* (emphasis quoted).[83]

RBJ was always very proud of his association with INS. It was easy to see why, because getting the story out first over the wires was the kind of intensely competitive journalism that he loved. It is obvious from his previous athletic and newspaper careers that winning under intense and public competition came naturally to him. This most likely is why he preferred to return to INS in his later career rather than edit the *Deseret News* in Salt Lake City - which goals at that time were not based on competition for the "scoop" - and why he cherished his experience as a war correspondent in World War II. The career record of INS "scoops" in the 1930s was respectable. Some of these were:

September 25, 1934 - I.N.S. scored one of the most notable beats ever recorded by any press association on the arrest of the Lindbergh kidnaping suspect, Bruno Richard Hauptmann.

October 2, 1935 - I.N.S. three hours ahead on the first actual fighting in the Italo-Ethiopian war.

February 18, 1935 - The Supreme Court's momentous gold decision: I.N.S. was first and right. The ruling was misinterpreted, erroneously reported by others; I.N.S. was the only service to have it one hundred percent right from the first and was fifteen minutes ahead with the news.

October 9, 1934 - I.N.S. 25 minutes ahead on the assassinations of King Alexander of Jugoslavia and Foreign Minister Barthou of France at Marseilles.

May 28, 1935 - The Supreme Court wipes out the N.S.A. I.N.S. had cleared a complete story from Washington while opposition services were still fumbling with bulletins.

August 26, 1935 - The Rogers-Post airplane tragedy; first definite confirmation of crash and deaths comes from I.N.S.

February 13, 1935 - Hauptmann death sentence verdict; I.N.S. first and accurate. Opposition service erroneously reported sentence to life imprisonment.

February 14, 1935 - Hauptmann breaks his silence; his first interview for publication is obtained by James L. Kilgallen, I.N.S. star, in an I.N.S. exclusive.

July 24, 1934 - Exclusive story by Jack Lait, I.N.S. writer and internationally known author, revealed that the "woman in red" lured John Dillinger into G-men's death trap. Lait also revealed the name of the officer who actually fired the fatal shot.

October 22, 1934 - I.N.S. 45 minutes ahead on the capture of "Pretty Boy" Floyd.

July 25, 1934 - Delfs assassination. I.N.S. three hours ahead of other services.

December 1, 1932 - Exclusive by Edward Hunter, I.N.S. war correspondent in Manchuria, confirms the charges made by the Chinese government that 2,709 men, women and children had been "massacred" by Japanese troops in three Manchurian towns. I.N.S. sent Hunter to the scene to make a first-hand investigation when the Japanese government denied the Chinese charges. Hunter's history-making story was the answer and aroused tremendous world feeling.

November 24, 1934 - Dr. Alice Wynekoop at Chicago confesses that she killed her daughter-in-law. I.N.S. half-hour beat. This Chicago murder had been front page news all over the country and the confession was a tremendously big story.

June 10, 1932 - 45-minute beat on the suicide of Violet Sharpe, a suspect in the Lindbergh baby murder case and employed as a maid in the Englewood home of Mrs. Dwight W. Morrow.

October 10, 1932 - Samuel Insull, fallen utilities monarch, who had been sought by authorities of seven nations for a week, is found by the I.N.S. staff correspondent at Athens, Greece. Brilliant beat of 18 hours and an exclusive interview.[84]

The air of self-congratulation that is conveyed is not the important point; rather, this listing reflects the kind of working environment in which RBJ thrived. Furthermore, deriving from his journalistic origins as a sports reporter, he found that working for INS was also not uncongenial because INS had, by the mid-1930s, arguably the premier race-track quotation and sporting news communications system in the country. Much of this was centered on the Pacific Coast.[85]

By 1936 (when he returned to Los Angeles - and probably earlier than that), RBJ was very well-known in California newspaper, public relations, and political circles. His children never questioned - nor had reason to question - whether he would be a success professionally. He had already achieved that level of accomplishment. He also, by then, had established ties with the U.S. Navy which were to become a continuing source of satisfaction to him, and by World War II, had made him a more effective war correspondent. As he recalled: "I first saw the [USS] *Chicago* in 1932 when the press association for which I was working assigned me to cover the Fleet in spring maneuvers. These were long, involved problems and carried us from Southern California to Panama, thence to the West Indies and finally into New York. The Navy put me aboard the *Chicago* for my baptism into Fleet problems....Years later I sailed on the *Chicago* twice out of Pearl Harbor and we weren't on maneuvers. The United States and Japan were at war."[86]

The Oakland years were also among the happiest times in RBJ and Mary's marriage. They both were actively involved in the Oakland Ward, which embraced Berkeley and environs as well as the Piedmont and Rockridge sections of Oakland, where they lived at 6260 Broadway Terrace.[87] RBJ was a Counselor in the bishopric, and Mary was President of the Ward Relief Society. At the conclusion of her service, Mary was presented by the women of her Relief Society board a hand-made quilt with their names embroidered on it as a token of their appreciation and as a remembrance. Mary and RBJ made some lifelong friends during this period: Mary and Elden Rex, LaVerne and Delbert Rock, and Dorothy and Leslie Stone come to mind. One important reason why these friendships formed and endured was that they all had served in the Oakland Ward Bishopric together at one time or another.

Rockridge house

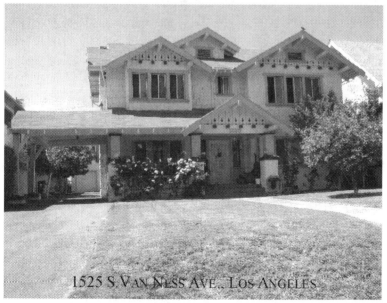

1525 S. Van Ness Ave., Los Angeles

Van Ness house

Mary's 7-passenger Buick

Fred, Burdette, Mary Ellen, Bill, Bob, 1941]

Wilshire Ward - Changing Times

The lure of the motion picture industry was irresistible to the Southern California Mormons of RBJ's generation: "...the fact that many Saints in this area were both affluent and influential, contributed to...attitudes and practices that were not necessarily common elsewhere in the Church."[88]

The neighborhood to which the family moved - called the West Wilshire District - was considered at that time to be part of a very desirable residential area. The house, at 1525 South Van Ness Avenue, was constructed before World War I, with shingles and masonry pillars in the popular California bungalow style. The neighborhood around Van Ness Avenue, between Pico and Venice Boulevards, was undergoing a transition from single-family homes to multi-family. Some "old families" remained there, but they were mostly widows. Some "new families," which included RBJ and Mary's clan, were replacing them. The trend seemed to be toward newer, smaller families which occupied the four-unit apartment houses or the converted homes. The entire area could still be considered upper-middle to middle class, with virtually no ethnic mixing, but there were already clear indications that the area was becoming more middle to lower-middle class, and that the ethnic mix would eventually include Asians and Hispanics and some Afro-Americans.

The home was near Wilshire Ward, located at 1209 South Manhattan Place, on the corner of Country Club Drive, between Pico and Olympic Boulevards.[89] One reason for RBJ's selection of a house on South Van Ness was that it was not far from the ward. Even before they returned to Los Angeles, RBJ and Mary were very familiar with Wilshire Ward, having assisted in its construction in 1927. The men who were involved with RBJ in the ward - or earlier, for that matter, in the Adams Ward - were in some cases the same men who re-appeared later in his life when the family attended the Beverly Hills Ward.

In its early days, the influence of Hollywood and the motion picture industry extended to the careers of many Mormons, and not just RBJ's. For this reason, the fact that RBJ had been deeply embroiled in the lives and careers (and scandals) of well-known celebrities in the 1920s and early 1930s, was not as remarkable as one might think - and certainly not incompatible with "respectable" Church membership. Some of those names included the first bishop of Wilshire Ward, David P. Howells, and Lionel C. Banks, Daken Broadhead, Laraine Day, Rhonda Fleming, Orson H. Hewlett, Mead H. Horton, Jr., the King Sisters (Driggs family), Dr. Vern O. Knudsen, Robert Major, Moroni Olsen, Charles B. Stewart, Sr., the Whitaker family, and Norma Jean Wright. Mormons who were making their way in the performing arts, and the attendant supporting activities, such as public relations, acoustical and set design, dance and music schools, real estate, law, and insurance were also those who were in the leadership positions of the local Church.[90]

Wilshire Ward, side

Wilshire Ward, front

In fact, the entire issue of Hollywood/Church influences was played out in the planning, construction, and use of Wilshire Ward: "President McCune believed not only that the Saints in the Hollywood Stake were entitled to the finest facilities available, but also that their activities should be worthy of the chapel he envisioned and in the best of taste and, at times, even elegant...A rumor even circulated in Salt Lake City that the General Authorities should take tuxedos with them when visiting the Hollywood Stake. This rumor actually had some basis in fact, for many Church social activities, especially those involving stake leaders, were formal affairs requiring tuxedos for men and [long] gowns for women.[91]

Nonetheless, the General Authorities were becoming uneasy with this style, and in April 1931, President McCune was unexpectedly released as President of the (then) Hollywood Stake.[92] Some members of the Stake High Council apparently thought that his removal was because of the high construction cost of Wilshire Ward, and they protested. Others felt that he was being mistreated because he learned of his imminent removal indirectly, rather than officially from his leaders before the change occurred. In fact, in late December 1929, LeGrand Richards, who succeeded President McCune, had specifically been called by President Heber J. Grant to go to California to become the stake president." As one person put it: "...the new stake president felt that changes were needed in attitude, organization, and social patterns..."[93] Another said it more bluntly: "Prior to President Richards' administration, some of the Brethren in Salt Lake City had criticized the Stake for a tendency toward elitism. Parties for stake officers, for example, often reflected the social status of some stake members. Many were held in the beautiful lounge at the stake center and formal dress was required. Other instances of somewhat exclusive social activities were suggested in the organization of special clubs by wives of stake leaders."[94] Wilshire Ward, still today an architectural landmark, became the Stake Center on November 19, 1939, when the Los Angeles Stake was carved out of the former Hollywood Stake.[95] Included in the new Stake were the Adams, Arlington, Beverly Hills, Hollywood, and Wilshire Wards.

Thus, the tie between the "glamour" of Hollywood and the reflected social nature of the local Mormon community in Southern California was being loosened even before the mid-1930s, when RBJ and Mary returned there. It is interesting to note, however, that the same persons who provided the leadership before this change also provided the leadership afterward. What differed were not the people, but the attitudes. There was more an egalitarian sense to worship and social activities, and a greater emphasis on the spiritual, rather than the material, aspects of living.[96] For RBJ and Mary, this could not help but be an advantage, although they doubtless had enjoyed the social pattern that had existed at the time that they had moved to Northern California. They now had a large half-grown family with which to cope, and inevitably their considerations as to what was important in their domestic life changed accordingly.

Publicity and Metro-Goldwyn-Mayer (MGM)

As the fateful 1940s began, RBJ renewed his association with Ralph Wheelwright, who had been with him at the *Los Angeles*

Examiner, and who had covered the Aimee Semple McPherson disappearance for the *Examiner*. Following the McPherson disappearance, Hearst had assigned Wheelwright to handle the publicity for Marion Davies, a long-time very close friend of Hearst. In 1930, Wheelwright became Assistant Director of Publicity at MGM; he worked under Howard Strickling, and was in that position until 1943, when he became a member of the studio writing department.[97]

Wheelwright's career paralleled RBJ's in several important respects. They came from humble backgrounds, made their way up the career ladder through reporting, served in and around Los Angeles in public relations, and then finally in June 1941 became colleagues again, this time at MGM. Publicity and public relations, as far as the movie industry is concerned, are virtually inseparable. If a distinction must be made, it might be that publicity applies to individuals, and public relations to institutions. The job of the MGM publicity department, therefore, was primarily to promote individual would-be or reigning stars.[98] In other words: "In Hollywood's heyday, studios in league with reporters and editors (who were sometimes paid off) kept scandals quiet."[99] When a star got into a moral or legal predicament, the first rescue calls went to the studio, and that usually meant the publicity department would act. Promotion for the pictures themselves was handled from New York; the task of the publicity department at MGM was primarily either "image-making" or "damage control" in dealing with the large contingent of reporters located in Los Angeles and Hollywood whose only job was to report on the movie industry. In many of the memoirs of the MGM stars of this period, the name of Howard Strickling appears, for very good reason - he was Director of Publicity.

RBJ and Wheelwright performed the same services. "In days to come when Louis B. Mayer or Jean Harlow or Tyrone Power had to make decisions that might affect their careers they would have the infallible advice of Howard Strickling or Harry Brand..."[100]Mayer kept a close eye on his stars: "To encourage his actors to walk the straight-and-narrow, he was lavish with his advice on love, marriage, family planning and divorce, the gist of the advice being: (1) think before you leap into bed; (2) remember that there is a time and place for everything; (3) what is good for the heart and the loins is not necessarily good for the career."[101]

MGM Studios

RBJ and Mary at MGM party

RBJ was not unfamiliar with Louis B. Mayer because, as an executive with William Randolph Hearst, he had witnessed firsthand how these two "moguls" had manipulated the California gubernatorial election of 1934. In that election, the two joined forces to defeat Upton Sinclair, the Democratic candidate, against the candidacies of Frank E. Merriam, the Republican, and Raymond Haight, the Independent. To end the threat of more taxes on the movie industry, and "socialistic programs": "Louis B. Mayer of MGM, Republican State Committee vice-chairman, commanded the Hollywood sector; William Randolph Hearst hastened home from Bad Nauheim, Germany, to marshal his newspapers for the fight."[102] With an unprecedentedly tendentious campaign organized by both Hearst and Mayer, Sinclair lost, and Merriam won.[103] It is widely acknowledged that that election ushered in the era of Hollywood's entry into politics, which was to include, unfortunately, the infamous McCarthy period of the late 1940s, when many eminent professionals in the movie industry had their careers smeared, crippled or terminated.

The other losing candidate, Raymond Haight, was a prominent Los Angeles attorney and Republican political figure whose son, Raymond, Jr., married RBJ and Mary's only daughter, Mary Ellen in 1948, thus joining two families the heads of which had been intimately involved in the public life of Los Angeles - and California in general - for over two decades. Although the members of this branch of the Haight family were not Mormons, they descended from the same pioneers who crossed the Rockies, one branch going on to Oregon, and the other turning south to Utah where they converted to Mormonism. A very distant cousin of Ray's, David B. Haight, served as an apostle in the Council of the Twelve of The Church of Jesus Christ of Latter-day Saints.[104]

The constant drama that went on both before and behind the cameras spilled over into their home life primarily because Mary and RBJ would have free tickets to all of the film premiers and other events, such as the Academy Awards ceremony. At Christmas, they received lavish gifts - often liquor, which was given away - and the children were invited to the birthday parties of such child stars as Shirley Temple. On the other hand, RBJ disapproved when Fred and Burdette skirted on the fringes of the "extras" world. He did not want his children to become involved in the movie industry. Although his career had been full of famous highlights that came to him through journalism and public relations, RBJ wanted them to benefit from his success by entering into what to him were considered the more "respectable" professions. The children doubtless enjoyed the derivative exposure, as did many of their friends.

RBJ claimed that he left INS for MGM because of the money - his family, as it grew, was indeed costing more - but in fact he did not dislike this kind of work - he enjoyed the celebrity of the movie industry. But, over time, publicity work was bound to become repetitious regardless of the fame of one's "clients." Hollywood personalities, in spite of Louella Parsons' breathless treatment of them, can grow stale if one gets to know them too well. In contrast, the new and unexpected was the norm in RBJ's newspaper and wire service endeavors.

It is one thing for a journalist to get a real "scoop," and another for a journalist to get a manufactured "scoop." It was the responsibility of the studio publicity departments to control and to manipulate what the large Hollywood press corps heard and received.[105] RBJ preferred uncovering the real thing, rather than manufacturing something to be fed to the Hollywood press corps. The advent of World War II gave him the opportunity to return to his first love with a vengeance.

Chapter Four

RBJ GOES TO WAR: 1941-1942

"I shall return."

The Initial War at Sea

On Sunday morning, December 7, 1941, RBJ drove out to the San
Fernando Valley to ride his horse, which was stabled there. The
rest of the family went to church as usual. When they returned
home, they learned that RBJ had already been contacted by INS
from New York to cover the bombing of Pearl Harbor. He left
for San Francisco that day on a leave of absence from MGM, and
was soon aboard a Navy flight bound for Hawaii; he was one of
the first journalists from the mainland to arrive in Pearl Harbor
after the disaster. RBJ's activities in the early stages of the Pacific
war were described:

> Joining U.S. correspondents in Australia during
> the early period were Tom Yarbrough, A.P.,
> formerly in London and Honolulu; Don Caswell,
> UP; Ralph Jordan, INS; Theodore H. White,
> *Time*; Hanson W. Baldwin, military and naval
> correspondent for the *New York Times*; Robert
> J. Doyle, *Milwaukee Journal*; and William M.
> (Bill) Henry, Los Angeles Times....There were new

arrivals, but others who had come to observe the first activities in the area left on other assignments. Some who had come from the United States returned there, at least temporarily, including Knickerbocker, Harsch, Lardner, Angly, and Jordan....[106]

RBJ recalled in 1943 his association with H. R. Knickerbocker - his admiration for Knickerbocker was longstanding, and reflects how those correspondents covering the war regarded themselves as members of a fraternity:

> One day shortly after the Pearl Harbor disaster I was standing in the lobby of the Alexander Young Hotel in Honolulu wondering when "Knick" would appear, for he was bound to be along shortly with a story like the Pacific war getting under way. He appeared at once, said, 'Let's go,' and we went, with task forces of the Pacific Fleet, with the Jap-destroying American aviators at Port Darwin, with General MacArthur in Australia, with the Australians and Americans in New Guinea, with Gen. Patrick J. Hurley in New Zealand. Between "Knick" and the war there never was a dull moment.

> ...When I was Pacific Coast news manager for International News Service our biggest name writer was Knickerbocker. Papers bought the service just to get "Knick." He now is with the Chicago Sun, or was the last time I saw him, which was when we landed on the West Coast from the Southwest Pacific theater of war....He not only is known to all the newspaper reading public and is just as well known incidentally in Europe and Australia as in the United States, but

he is a newspaperman's reporter, admired, and respected and sought after by members of his own profession.[107]

After arriving in Hawaii, RBJ was instructed to "...go with fleet wherever action likeliest regardless distance."[108] He was authorized to go with the *Chicago* by Waldo Drake, who was an old Los Angeles friend, and who later returned to the *Los Angeles Times*. The authorizing letter said: "The bearer of this note, Mr. Ralph Jordan, accredited correspondent of the International News Service, has been granted authority by the Commander-in-Chief, United States Pacific Fleet, in an official letter addressed to the Commanding Officer, USS CHICAGO dated January 5, 1942, to take passage in the CHICAGO during her first available scheduled operating period." [109]

He immediately sailed from Pearl Harbor with a naval task force that included the carrier *Enterprise*. The *Enterprise* had escaped the Japanese attack because it had been secretly steaming toward Wake Island to replenish the island's supply of fighter aircraft. Under the command of Admiral William "Bull" Halsey, Task Force 2, known as the *Enterprise* force, returned to Pearl Harbor and was assigned to find enemy submarines. Mary claimed that the task force destroyed the first two Japanese submarines in the war. But she was to be proven wrong, as were the flyers on that cruise who had reported Japanese submarine soundings and sinkings.[110]

It is noteworthy that RBJ was present when a fundamental change in American naval strategy occurred: "...Admirals King, Nimitz, and William Halsey...took the fleet's Battle Force and Scouting Force and reorganized them into several Task Forces, each with a carrier at its core. That ended the doctrine of the indivisibility of the battle fleet and the centrality of the battleship."[111] The naval historian Marc Milner put it: "...the USN blossomed into a Service built around large carriers with large air wings embarked. As in the European theatre, battleships soon took on a lone and almost brooding character, forming the 'base' upon which carrier air power rested... ." [112]

In January, 1942, RBJ was listed as a "Staff Correspondent, International News [Service]" from "Aboard a Man-O'-War with the U.S. Pacific Fleet." In a bylined story dated January 22, he reported:

> You could have knocked a few eyes off with a stick the way they were popping - that's how amazed the officers and men were - had you been aboard the heavy cruiser from which this dispatch is being written. This correspondent with several of the ships personnel was standing at the rail of our big fighting craft as she ploughed through the Far Western waters searching for Japanese or other hostile forces and occasionally doing a little business. We were looking at a vessel accompanying us. She wasn't much farther away than a small boy could hurl a rock with a good slingshot. She was sailing along beautifully and made a beautiful picture of power and might silhouetted against the setting sun. From inside our ship a radio was blaring. It had picked up a Tokyo short wave broadcast and this was what we heard, word for word: 'We sympathize with the United States upon the loss of the huge aircraft carrier Lexington, the greatest carrier in the world. First it was the Langley...next the Enterprise and then the Lexington. Now there is only the Saratoga left. 'Eyes popped at that assertion because the ship we were watching was none other than the Lexington. And if she were lost, she certainly didn't know it and didn't act like it.[113]

It is interesting to compare RBJ's writing style, honed over many years of reporting major news stories, to that of an historian's many years later about the same event:

> Halsey was aboard the Big E, so he knew she hadn't been sunk by any means. The *Lexington* was ploughing along, big, tough, unharmed, in another task force, and those aboard who also heard the news were aware she was no Flying Dutchman come back from a watery grave to plague sailormen in the dark of the night. The *Saratoga* was in dry dock at Pearl Harbor, with a torpedo in her innards, but this was only a temporary indisposition, and she soon would be back at her old stand. The *Langley* was en route to the South Pacific. Thus, while the Jap communiqué was impressive, it was exactly a hundred per cent false, and the Imperial Navy, of course, knew it.[114]

* * * * *

> In the Pacific in March 1942, the Navy had three carriers - the *Enterprise* and the *Lexington*, fortuitously safely out to sea during the Pearl Harbor raid, and the *Yorktown*, recently arrived from the Atlantic. The *Saratoga* had been torpedoed in January and was out of operation for five months. The *Hornet* arrived in April. That was all that was available for taking on the main arm of the Japanese naval offensive.[115]

MacArthur and the Beginning of the Road Back

RBJ was accredited later to the staff of General Douglas MacArthur as he began the march back through the Southwest Pacific. When

MacArthur moved his headquarters from Brisbane, Australia, to Port Moresby, New Guinea, RBJ was in the press entourage that followed. Doubtless it was in New Guinea where he contracted the malaria and dengue fever that eventually forced him to leave the war zone and INS. This changed his life profoundly. As reported by General George C. Kenney, the commander of the Army Air Forces (Fifth AF) assigned to MacArthur: "When the Americans first came to New Guinea and saw the Aussies wearing shorts and shirtsleeves cut off above the elbow, it appealed to them as a smart idea for that hot, humid, jungle service. Just as an experiment, I put long trousers and long-sleeved shirts on one squadron of a fighter group and shorts and short-sleeved shirts on another squadron for a month. At the end of the trial period, I had two cases of malaria in the long-trousered, long-sleeved squadron and sixty-two cases in the squadron wearing shorts."[116] Later, Kenney observed that the Australians also reverted to long trousers and shirts. Given RBJ's admiration of the Australians, he most probably would have initially worn short trousers and shirts, too. In March, RBJ reported other observations "With United Nations Forces in the Southwest Pacific":

> Contrary to the usually exaggerated claims of Japan, all American forces assigned to the defense of Java [Dutch East Indies] made their way successfully from that embattled isle before the enemy overran it, this correspondent is able to reveal today. Tokyo's announcement that 5,000 British, Australian and United States troops 'surrendered' upon the occupation of Banding is erroneous in this report at least....I can say positively on unquestioned authority that the Tokyo communiqué was wrong on these points: The Dutch never had more than three or four divisions of 12,000 each in Java and 75 per cent of these were natives, while the Dutch air force

> consisted of only sixty or seventy fighters and thirty or forty bombers, but friends of mine who were there say those Dutch took a frightful toll with each plane.

> I can say that no American troops surrendered in Java because all got out and there never were more than 600 there, all air force personnel.[117]

Stylistically, he reported in the first person and anecdotally. This is in the tradition of war reporting stretching back at least as far as the Crimean War, and it helped such men as Winston Churchill and Richard Harding Davis to gain fame at an early age. Noticeably, RBJ was allowed to report authoritatively by his censors in order to rebut Japanese propaganda claims. In other words, his was not unbiased reporting, but it certainly was the type of reportage that suited his personality and temperament. RBJ left it to others, including the large public information staffs of the various military headquarters, to file the impersonal, detached, facts-only stories.

But it is difficult to imagine that *any* story from MacArthur's headquarters could be wholly "objective": "...although the General had told war correspondents that they were free to write anything they pleased about him, [chief press officer Le Grande A.] Diller censored all criticism from their stories. They were not permitted to find fault with anything - strategy, tactics, morale, food, supplies, or, above all, the theater's commander in chief."[118] The "Somewhere in Australia" identification that was used for these dispatches was a euphemism for a story emanating from MacArthur's headquarters. Also, a reference to "authoritative military and civilian circles" usually meant that the story was one that met with MacArthur's staff's approval - *i.e.* reflected favorably on MacArthur. Obviously, RBJ was one of those war correspondents who were in the General's good graces.

Here are two more examples of RBJ's reportage:

[Headlined "From the Jaws of Death" Isle Aborigines Save Yank Flier: Somewhere in Australia] - A luncheon with a crowd of American fighter pilots who have been doing such valiant work in the battle for northern Australia today produced one of the most spectacular stories of the war. It concerns the hair raising adventure of Second Lieutenant Clarence S. Sanford of Auburn, N.Y., whose life was saved a half dozen times in a series of near miracles. About a month ago he and several American pals were flying over the Pacific, some distance from their base, when they sighted a flight of several Japanese bombers escorted by nine Zero fighters, and took after them. His plane was disabled, and he bailed out in his lifejacket about three miles offshore. Sanford's jacket, however, failed him and he stripped off all his clothes and started to swim, barely reaching the beach, where he collapsed. He does not know how long he was unconscious, but when he came to he found two aborigines, native blacks, who are particularly wild in this area, standing over him with spears pricking his chest. One of the aborigines asked in broken English: 'You Jap?' The spears pinned him tighter to the sand, and Sanford cried: 'No, I am an American.' He wore a tiny silver crucifix on a chain around his neck, symbol of his faith. As Sanford spoke, the native's eyes rested on the cross, his black face brightened and the aborigine, pointing to the crucifix, said: 'Jesus number one man.' From potential killers the natives turned at once to super kindness. They explained that Sanford was on Bremer Island, off the Australian coast, and that they visited the shore where they found him only once a week to fish. The nearest habitation, a mission, was 25 miles away. The natives then helped the nude Sanford through the blazing sun for those long, terrible miles, and he arrived at the mission fearfully burned. Here he stayed for two weeks under their care. When he needed expert medical treatment, another near miracle occurred. A little inter-island sailing lugger showed up, although its schedule was only once a month or thereabouts. Sanford was landed at the tiny port of Millingimbi, Australia, recovered, and is now back looking for more action against the Japs, proudly showing beads and other trinkets given him by two of his black friends as tokens of their esteem and for good luck.[119]

* * * * *

[Headlined 'Teamwork Foils Jap Air Victory,' An Advanced United Nations Base Somewhere in the South Pacific, April 28 (INS)] - This base, at present, is the hottest spot in the southwest Pacific combat zone, and an absorbing drama, played here only a few minutes ago, demonstrates why the Japanese are losing control of the air throughout this area. The story of that drama is one which shows the value of teamwork and aggressive spirit. Characters are an Australian fighter pilot in an American plane, an American machine gunner on a little American freighter, and a Japanese pilot in a Zero fighter. Two of them I know - the Aussie pilot, a quiet blond from Brisbane and the stocky little machine gunner from Omaha. I arrived at this feverish tropical island port on a freighter and watched that stocky machine gunner for several afternoons, polishing up the mechanism of his gun like a watchmaker with a fine timepiece, and obviously aching for a chance to use it. When the chance came, he was old Dead Eye Dick himself, and that is why the Aussie pilot is alive to fly another day and the Jap pilot dead and laid to rest on a grassy hillside. It was just like having a gallery seat at a play. Into the little mountain-enclosed harbor lying directly opposite me came the Aussie in a Kittyhawk, as American P-40 fighter planes are known here. He was in a big hurry and the reason was his ammunition was gone. And right behind him, over the same hill, flashed a Japanese Zero. The Jap was on the Kittyhawk's tail and his guns were all barking, with tracers flying around the 'Kitty' like illuminated hornets. The Aussie was twisting and turning the 'Kitty' a terrific speed just above the water, but he was unable to shake off the Jap, who got in a burst which seemed to knock the American ship sideways, but not out. The 'Kitty' banked suddenly and dived toward the freighter in the harbor. The Jap closed in fast for the kill. Then the stocky little machine gunner from Omaha, after letting the 'Kitty' go past his perch on the freighter, whammed a burst right into the Zero, which zoomed up, curved back and headed for home. It was too late. The Jap plane staggered across the bay and crashed into a hill. The 'Kitty,' unfortunately, was too badly hit to pull out of the glide and dropped into the water, but the pilot climbed out uninjured, and swam ashore.[120]

RBJ and two other correspondents were the first to enter Port Moresby after the Japanese attempt to capture it by land had failed (he had been in Darwin earlier.) RBJ reported the subsequent Japanese attempt to capture Port Moresby by sea, resulting in April-May 1942, in the Battle of the Coral Sea.[121]

Dispatch from the South Pacific, 1942

RBJ in the Pacific

He came away from the Pacific with a deep-seated admiration for General MacArthur.[122] In fact, RBJ wore his stiff-brimmed officers' cap in the same crushed fashion affected by MacArthur from as far back as World War I. MacArthur's histrionics and florid rhetoric apparently did not repel RBJ, as they did many other correspondents. Being himself a person that enjoyed the dramatic and engaged in hyperbole in his writings, he was obviously at ease writing about a man of similar temperament who was, at the same time, the nearest thing to a national hero that America possessed at this bleak time in its war with the Axis Powers. RBJ doubtless was in the room when MacArthur held his famous press conference to announce his intention to defend Australia from New Guinea: "...the thirty or more war correspondents and officers rose as the General made an impressive entry - bare-headed, grave, distinguished looking, immaculate. His right arm was raised in salute. There was no other introduction. Pacing to and fro...MacArthur immediately began to declaim his statement of the military situation. His phrasing was perfect, his speech clear and unhalting, except for pauses for dramatic emphasis;

the correspondents took notes, but there was no interruption of any kind. The conference room had become a stage. MacArthur the virtuoso, the other officers the 'extras' in the cast, and the correspondents the audience. It was a dramatic occasion."[123]

RBJ described some years later his first impression of MacArthur:

> Only a few American correspondents had been with him in the Philippines. They had known him for some time and were his friends. This day in Melbourne he was really stepping onto the world stage for the first time, stepping out before the men who represented the press and radio of the world, the men through whose eyes he would be represented everywhere, whose opinions of him would eventually be reflected wherever people could read or hear. This was a critical audience gathered for his first press conference in Australia.
>
> How would he meet this test I wondered and hoped, as an American that our great hero would not let us down, especially before the foreign writers and broadcasters. But I acknowledged to myself, the chances were against him, very much against him. These men were not easily impressed. The general couldn't have picked a tougher jury. Most of these men, in fact, had never been overly impressed by anybody or anything. The world and its scintillating characters had paraded past them, and generally speaking, had left them cold. Most heroes were just overrated jerks to them.
>
> I looked around the waiting crowd...None of the reportorial crowd ever had talked with MacArthur before. Few had ever seen him. The general was

completely on his own, starting fresh, with no prejudices either for or against him. The glowing press notices he had received meant nothing here. There was a stir at the door and the general entered, accompanied by Col. Larry Lehrman, formerly an Associated Press correspondent in Washington, now doing a swell job of public relations on MacArthur's staff. Straight as an arrow, his lips and eyes steady, his face showing little trace of the fierce ordeal he had been through in the Philippines, the general strode quickly to a desk at one end of the big room, as we all gathered around him, were introduced to him by Lehrman (a couple of us had met him the day before at the Melbourne railroad station), and he started to talk.

'Gentlemen,' he said, 'you would, of course, like to know how we are going to win the war. Well, I'll tell you.' And tell us he did, while the press of the world examined him carefully and prepared to pass judgment.[124]

At the risk of overdoing it, here is a column RBJ wrote that expanded on this press conference, because it shows even more clearly how RBJ could write with a great dramatic sense about a master dramatist. In this respect, recalling the brilliant theatrics of Aimee Semple McPherson, it is not difficult to fathom RBJ's own instincts and fascination with high drama - highly publicized:

General Douglas MacArthur rose from the desk in his headquarters in Melbourne, Australia, and faced the battery of war correspondents representing all the English-speaking peoples of the world, and the Latin-American countries of Central and South America. It was an important moment for the general: his first press conference since his escape from the Philippines. The impressions of these men, by press and radio, would portray him everywhere. He stood tall, straight and fearless, looked us directly in the eye and told us how we could win the war with Japan. That is, he told us in response to a question. 'General,' said one of the correspondents, 'do you feel that Japan will prove a really tough nut to crack? And how are we going to whip the Japs?' MacArthur's eyes blazed. He has fiery dark eyes. His whole face grew taut. He snapped out his answer. His words fairly stung.

'There are no tougher people on earth,' he said, 'than the Japs. To whip them will be a tough problem, and that is putting it very gently and mildly.' Then the general strode back and forth in front of his desk, his head lowered thoughtfully. Raising his eyes after a moment, he continued: 'Of course, gentlemen, you'd like to know how we are going to win this war. Well, I'll tell you.'

Now his voice was hard and brittle and penetrating. His fists were clenched. His lips were drawn tightly over his teeth. He was the spirit of Bataan; the fighter, the killer. 'We'll only whip the Japanese,' he said, 'by killing them. We've got to kill them wherever we can find them. We've got to seek them out and kill them. Kill them in New Guinea, at Rabaul, in the Philippines, in Java, China, Burma and in Japan - yes, in Japan especially.' His hatred for the enemy in the Pacific was like a fire. It burned all of us who were listening to him. We unconsciously were lifted up with a great hatred too...[The correspondents] all,

71

in one way or another, declared that MacArthur was terrific. He had sold to the hilt the jury of press and radio.

> When I shut my eyes all I can see is MacArthur and an army of young Americans sweeping through Japan like avenging angels, with Japanese pierced by bayonets and blasted by shells, falling like leaves in a forest before an Autumn gale. He'd love it.[125]

RBJ had already had a career working with and writing about such noted practitioners of the dramatic as William Randolph Hearst, Louis B. Mayer, Aimee Semple McPherson, and the stars at MGM. He was in his element.

Being with MacArthur was, undoubtedly, the high point of his career.[126] It combined his love of being around military figures - the more colorful the better - with the excitement of combat reminiscent of his earlier days writing about and playing contact sports. War, to him, as it was to MacArthur, was both heroic and sordid. Both RBJ and MacArthur were romantics - they viewed the (perhaps somewhat imagined) past as the model for the present. The bestiality of combat - and in New Guinea it was as bestial as it could get - was compensated for by the heroism of those valiant soldiers who either died in glory or who survived in honor.

Nonetheless, he also approved of Eisenhower, who was not nearly as colorful. He recounted a conversation on the subject of the two generals with approval: " 'Do you think,' I inquired, 'that Eisenhower is as good as MacArthur?' The two [senior] officers considered carefully: this was their reply. 'Yes, in some ways Eisenhower is a better commander than MacArthur, although the latter may be superior in his own special field. However, were I building an army I would just as soon have Eisenhower as chief as any officer in the world. He'll do a great job, that's certain.' "[127]

For the rest of his life, RBJ's greatest enjoyment was in recounting tales of the heroism and the brutality of war, as culled from episodes from his own experience in the Southwest Pacific. But he did not write or recount with approval; rather he wrote from a conviction that "gilding the lily" accomplishes nothing. As he put it: "I can see no purpose in twisting the truth, in war or peace....of underestimating our enemies...of looking at everything through rose-colored glasses. Let's try to see everything just as it is....we certainly are mature enough to expend our best efforts...to fight either on the battlefront or the home-front with complete concentration...without childish propaganda about how easily we whip our enemies."[128] His feelings were strong on this subject:

> Some of the news items that filter back from the battle fronts first make you gasp in amazement, then wonder what in the world they think our people are back here at home...children? Or nit-wits? For instance a press association dispatch ... from a United States Bomber Station in England, said that a group of our bombers roared over Europe and back to their field in England, without dropping their bombs...because the sky was overcast, they couldn't see their target clearly and they didn't want to take chances on killing civilians with inaccurate bombing. Isn't that a sweet thought: Bunk! The Germans bombed English cities mercilessly and the English have won everlasting fame by their night bombing of German cities, flying by instrument to their targets, and hitting not only military objectives but anything including homes, schools and hospitals, that happened to be in the vicinity.
>
> Any attempt to make war anything but what it is - brutal, bitter and vicious - gives me a pain. The blasting of the German dams, flooding densely populated areas, killing thousands of women and children, is an excellent example. I don't question

that these things are a military necessity...a nation at war, fighting for its very life, is justified, I suppose, in leveling any blow at an enemy that will inflict damage and tend toward victory...but why all the bunk we are fed?[129]

It is regrettable that RBJ's approach was not followed during the years when his government was dissembling to the American people about its Vietnam intervention and in its secret bombing of Cambodia. But RBJ approved of the atomic bombing of Japan, and would not have understood fifty years later the argument concerning both the efficacy and the morality of using this new devastating instrument of war to bring about the ultimate defeat of Japan. He would have remembered how unspeakably vicious and "inhumane" the war in the Pacific had been.

RBJ admired another colorful figure, Patrick J. Hurley, at that time Ambassador to New Zealand. Hurley played a far more important role in the formulation and execution of foreign policy at this time in his career than later, having been a familiar Washington figure who was close to President Roosevelt.[130] RBJ reported:

Headlined, 'MacArthur Plans Early Offensive,' General Douglas MacArthur's Headquarters, Australia, March 19 (INS). - General Douglas MacArthur's paramount purpose is to 'organize as rapidly as possible an offensive force for the eventual defeat of Japan and the relief of the beleaguered Philippine garrison,' Brigadier General Patrick Hurley, United States minister to New Zealand, disclosed today. Hurley, former United States secretary of war, returned to headquarters by plane after a conference with MacArthur to report that the general's aerial flight from the Bataan peninsula to Australia to become southwest Pacific commander of United Nations forces was one of the most spectacular in the

annals of military history....'General MacArthur
breathes the very spirit of victory,' Hurley said.[131]

Hurley and MacArthur were close at this time, being in
agreement on the military strategy needed to win in the Pacific,
which did not hurt Hurley's stature with RBJ. Hurley was also a
prominent Sigma Chi; neither would that diminish him in RBJ's
eyes. RBJ commented: "Tall, straight, interesting, colorful and
smart, he is nearing 70 years of age but thirsts for battle like a
young Viking....Hurley and MacArthur make a great pair."[132]

The easy, open camaraderie that went with wartime would
also have been congenial to RBJ. In a sense, the community of
war correspondents was not dissimilar to the masculine club life
that he had enjoyed while in college and later in journalism and
publicity. War correspondents themselves exercised a degree of
power and influence, reporting as they did on the activities of
both generals and their armies (or admirals and their navies)
which could not help but shape the images of not only who was
fighting the war, but also how it was being fought, and with what
results. "Correspondents tended to become involved in military
affairs...with some favored by commanding generals and chiefs
of staff, and so contributing to public opinion figuring in the
generals' own power struggle."[133]

The system of war reporting tended to favor the large press
associations as well as the largest of the leading metropolitan
newspapers: "However necessary it may have been, the 'limited
facilities' policy adopted by the military authorities in active theaters
usually worked to the advantage of the representatives of the larger
agencies. The associations considered it a service to their clients to
offer 'undated lead' material along with other counsel designed to
help appraise the news. The role of the press associations in shaping
the end product in news was one of incalculable importance."[134]

The stories, however, had to be kept within certain limits
set by rules of censorship. For example, while he was aboard the
Chicago, RBJ was admonished: "...You are informed that this

command will be unable to release any articles written by you and that such articles should be submitted to the Commander-in-Chief, U.S. Pacific Fleet for censorship and release or to other competent U.S. Naval authority in accordance with existing security instructions prescribed by the Secretary of the Navy." The letter continued: "You are requested not to release for publication or through conversation or in any other manner (except to officers of the U.S. Navy or of the British or British Commonwealth Naval Forces) information regarding the means of your conveyance to Suva until authorized to do so."[135]

Not unfairly, at times RBJ was skeptical of the efficacy of such limitations. For example, before the war, when he was on the *Chicago* on a cruise with the Pacific fleet, he had another kind of experience concerning war secrets: "We correspondents were told that we must not, under any circumstances, mention...or even think, if thinking could be avoided...of a new, super-secret weapon just installed on some of our ships....The super-secret weapon turned out to be the .30 caliber machine gun, a wicked weapon indeed... The fleet sailed into Balboa Harbor on the Pacific side of the canal, then transited the big ditch to Colon on the Atlantic side. In Colon I was ashore, being shown the sights by a friend who was editing a Panama newspaper. In a hotel lobby he introduced me to two officers from foreign war ships which happened to be in Panama at that time....Well, imagine my horror when one of these officers inquired casually, 'By the way, Mr. Jordan, how are those .30 caliber machine guns, such as you have on the *Chicago*, working out in actual firing practice?' I didn't answer, but somehow my regard for military secrets was lowered."[136]

Being intensely patriotic long before war had broken out, RBJ would not have found it difficult to adapt to the constrictions of wartime reporting even though, as with most of his journalist colleagues, he remained skeptical of their efficacy or even appropriateness under some circumstances. He did not, however, approve of soldiers' (or sailors') attempts to "beat" the censor: "Our censors claim our doughboys are suffering from 'code in the head.'...It isn't difficult to beat a censor, but it shouldn't be done....Play the game probably isn't the best way to refer to the problem...it isn't a game between them and the censors, but a duty for the security of our armed forces."[137] RBJ was concerned when correspondents filed patently false stories that later on, when all the facts were known, would make the stories (and those who filed them) look silly.

In any event, rules of censorship were better than those imposed during World War I. This does not mean that the stories were not considered glamorous - and by extension that the persons filing these stories were not themselves somewhat of celebrity status. While RBJ was in the Pacific, this was illustrated in November 1942, when MacArthur moved his advance base from Brisbane to Port Moresby, with RBJ in his entourage: "... thereafter [MacArthur] moved so rapidly between Brisbane and New Guinea that often two luncheon tables were set for him, fifteen hundred miles apart. War correspondents' stories about him were still datelined "Somewhere in Australia," however, and to tens of millions of Americans that phrase was invested with a glamour unequaled by news from any other theater of war until Eisenhower landed in North Africa on November 8. During [MacArthur's] first days down under, Australian journalists had been cautioned not to publish his name because word of his presence might reveal his whereabouts to the enemy. If they must refer to MacArthur, they were advised, they should write He, or Him, as though he were divine. This seemed perfectly natural to him, of course." [138]

From Australia, RBJ went to Port Darwin, a desolate place on the northern coast of Australia that was considered a possible landing-place for a Japanese invasion force. He described how he and his colleagues got there:

> Sleeping on the roof of the front porch of Mrs. O'Brien's Hotel South Australia in Adelaide and partaking of her excellent meals were

fully appreciated by we four American war correspondents, but we wanted to get to Port Darwin....We wanted plane rides, but the aircraft operating between Adelaide and Darwin belonged to the Guinea Airways and this company only sent one plane a day northward....for some mysterious reason the airways office manager didn't like us and was to blame for our inability to leave Adelaide. So, we sat ourselves down at our typewriters at the Hotel South Australia and composed telegrams to everyone we knew in the Commonwealth. We sent bitter messages to Prime Minister John Curtin, to the secretary for war, the secretary for labor, to Gen. Douglas MacArthur, to the Australian commander, to other American and Australian officers...That afternoon we got replies from all of them. They said we could count on their help...In the darkness of the next morning we strolled around to the airport and asked the airways office manager if he thought we could get out to Darwin. He looked coldly at us. In fact, he looked almost hatefully at us. Then he shook a sheaf of telegrams under our noses and shouted: 'I've got all these about you chaps, from practically everyone in Australia. You most certainly can get out this morning and I hope that nothing will happen to our plane, but if it must crash, I hope it is this morning. If I never see any of you again I will be quite happy.'[139]

As cited earlier, it was at Port Moresby that RBJ contracted with malaria and dengue fever, and had to be evacuated to Honolulu, and hence back to the United States for what he anticipated would be a resumption of his career at MGM. Possibly he was too old to be doing what he did - just as he was too young to be in World

War I. He described the conditions under which the American and Australian soldiers and airmen had to live and to fight:

> Our men who are fighting in New Guinea are faced with the most trying hardships. It is a terrible problem just to live on that tropical island, let alone do any fighting. When we American correspondents first got into New Guinea we found two Australian newspapermen who had been there for several months. They were living with the high command of the Australian army in a house which was comfortable enough for New Guinea but which would be scorned in America. The floor was about two feet off the ground, on pilings; the walls and roof were slabs of bark and through this bark the rain poured, or was whipped in on the wings of tropical hurricanes. The place was wet all the time, for with the exception of a small area immediately around Port Moresby, it rains constantly in New Guinea - not just rain; the skies flood, jungles drip and the ground is slippery with red mud.

> We moved in with the Aussies for a time. Their names were Stockton and White. Both wore nothing but tropical shorts and shoes, for a steam bath is a cool and refreshing experience compared with the heat of those headquarters, which for some mysterious reason were built in a pocket in the hills so no air from the sea could get in. The little defile was like an oven, confining the horrible heat.

> White was gaunt and apparently quite tired. He apologized and explained he had just recovered from malaria a month or so previously and was coming down with another attack. Stockton looked

like a patchwork quilt, the result of tropical rash, which he had with him always in New Guinea and couldn't cure. That will give you a faint idea of life and health on the island, not mentioning tropical dysentery, dengue fever and mosquitos. Everybody suffers from dysentery from time to time; the same goes for dengue fever, which is similar to the flu, except that it knocks its victims out faster, harder and longer. The mosquitos are an absolute scourge. They are big, strong, wicked and swarm to the attack night and day, forcing their way through head and bed nets.

We found it almost impossible to do any work. Just keeping alive occupied practically all of our energy and time, and we weren't doing any fighting. The combat troops down there never can be repaid, if they come out alive, for the hardships and suffering they have undergone. All the courtesies and consideration and kindness we can show them will not make up for their privations. They are wonderful men....[140]

A full year after his departure for the Pacific, a personal event occurred which added a larger and more ever-lasting perspective to the horrific events RBJ had witnessed during the war. On December 21, 1942, his Stake Patriarch, George T. Wride, laid hands on his head to pronounce a patriarchal blessing. His blessing said that "...thou shalt have a rare gift of discernment of Spirits and of understanding men and their purposes. Thou shalt not be deceived but shall be a master of circumstances and shall direct many into human activities and help to round out the world's work." RBJ certainly experienced fulfillment of this part of his blessing.

Chapter Five

AN EDITOR, AT LAST: THE DESERET NEWS - 1942-1943

"For nearly four years the *News* gave a move-by-move account of the most devastating war of all time."[141]

Editing the *Deseret News*

Not long after RBJ returned to MGM, Apostle Albert E. Bowen of the Mormon Church's ruling hierarchy, approached him about the possibility of coming to the *Deseret News*, the Church's daily newspaper and official organ, to serve as Managing Editor. Although Mary had her reservations about his returning to a much smaller career environment – and one in which the policies and politics of the dominant religion in Utah would be inescapably involved - RBJ apparently found it attractive. So within a few months after returning to MGM, he resigned to assume his new duties as of January 1, 1943. At the conclusion of the school year in mid-1943, the family moved to Salt Lake City, to join him. RBJ bought a fishing camp *Dunrovin'*, located on the Weber River, for the family's recreation (he loved stream fly-fishing).

Burdette, Fred, Mary Ellen, Bill, Bob, 1943
– en route to Dunrovin'

Dunrovin'

NEW EXECUTIVES OF THE DESERET NEWS—Newly appointed department heads of your daily paper are shown in these two pictures. Top, left to right, Ralph W. Jochim, managing editor; David A. Robinson, editor and assistant general manager; Jonathan Soen, promotion manager; and Donald A. S. Priestley, superintendent of the composing room. In the bottom picture are John A. Lewes, city circulation manager; J. Ralph Whitney, office manager; and Wilby M. Durham, circulation manager.

Six Executive Positions Filled
By Directors Of The Deseret News

Utahn In England Joins
Roosevelt Birthday Fete

The *Deseret News* Team

That he had commenced his newspaper career in Utah, and had become a well-known publicist and news correspondent are probably what made him an attractive prospect for the managing editor position. However, matters were complicated at the outset because RBJ was offered the job personally by Apostle Bowen, but he had not consulted with the General Manager, Mark E. Petersen who in fact would be RBJ's immediate superior.[142] Some years earlier, however, Petersen had said: "International News Service has been a most valuable asset to our paper. Through its special writers in particular it has been a stabilizing factor in our circulation and a builder of high reader interest. Writers such as Davis J. Walsh, Knickerbocker, Floyd Gibbons and Kilgallen have a wide following."[143] Thus, bringing to the *News* an INS executive would not have been an objectionable move *per se*.

RBJ's career as Managing Editor of the *Deseret News* proved short-lived, however, lasting only from January 1943 until April 1944. Simply put, circumstances in wartime Utah imposed financial and editorial constraints that could not be overcome, regardless of the aspirations of a Utah-bred "outsider."[144] Furthermore, his relationship with Petersen became increasingly uncomfortable. Clearly, Petersen was the ultimate insider: his entire career had been with the *News*, starting as a reporter in 1924, then copy reader, news editor, and managing editor. Furthermore, to underscore the sharp career differences between the two men, on April 6, 1944, after RBJ had departed for brighter prospects at INS headquarters in New York, Petersen was sustained an Apostle, and then in 1952 he became Chairman of the Board of Trustees of the Deseret News Publishing Company. Given the history of the governance of the *News*, which RBJ should have known, he miscalculated if his going to Utah was to give the *News* a more secular imprimatur without denying the nature of its ownership and the distinctive culture of its readership.

A crucial question might have been, for example, to what extent would RBJ have been able to influence the editorial policies when, in fact, he had no official responsibility over the editorial page. Many of the editorials originated at Church headquarters, and were "blue-penciled" by Petersen.[145] Furthermore, stories that would affect the Church's public image or that would be contrary to the political philosophy of the moment, could be delayed, revised, or withheld, and this would doubtless annoy him. Although a church-owned paper may not be as dependent on the goodwill of advertisers, this was also never far from the minds of the General Authorities – especially concerning the local news columns and editorial page.[146]

Although it would be foolish to suggest that someone like RBJ's former employer, William Randolph Hearst did not do the same thing with his newspapers, Hearst's papers were seen neither as representative of the "quality" press in America, nor as conventional home-town "respectability", two concepts which were important to the *News*. RBJ, of course, made his journalistic reputation practicing the Hearst kind of journalism; doubtless he had become accustomed to the Hearst style of newspapering, so he would have certainly understood the limitations in editorial freedom of the *News*.[147] Furthermore, as a practical matter, RBJ was not a "manager" by temperament. His gift, journalistically, was in finding a human-interest angle in a good news story. He could engage people far better than he could engage abstract issues, or what would today be considered "policy issues." Additionally: "Ralph learned rapidly that a lot of people of prominence knew better how to handle a newspaper than RBJ! He learned to roll with the punches and did so very well."[148] This was a lifelong trait.[149]

More to the point, even before the age of aggressive investigative journalism, the *News* had a "...musty (and somewhat undeserved) image... as a Church house organ that editorializes only along readily predictable, safely doctrinaire lines."[150] One observer commented that the editorials were "strong, confident" concerning "problems half a world away while hewing a safe line on local issues."[151] It is obvious, of course, that there need not be a conflict between religious ethics and journalistic ethics; it all depends on how broadly the two schools of ethics are defined. *Deseret News* Editor William Smart, who served in the 1970s, did not see the dilemma as insoluble, or even as incompatible, although in his tenure - as with any other editor's tenure - there were times of stress.[152]

RBJ had a low opinion of the graduates of journalism schools - even though he acknowledged that good schools of journalism existed, especially those at Columbia University, the University of Iowa, and Syracuse University. He was of the generation that believed that a good journalist learned his "craft" on the job. Labeling it a "profession," he felt, was elevating journalism to perhaps an excessively pompous status. He probably would have taken considerable interest in the career of Rod Decker, a *News* staffer of a later period who was described as: "A super-confident, breezily candid University of Utah graduate, [who] came to the *News* without a solid journalistic background. Decker went so far as to tell journalism classes and interviewers that he got his job because he knew Editor William Smart. Yet it became readily apparent that he *held* his job solely on merit."[153]

In this respect, RBJ was entirely in accord with his peers - John Lardner, Theodore H. White, H. L. Mencken, H. R. Knickerbocker, Adela Rogers St. Johns, James L. Kilgallen and his daughter Dorothy Kilgallen, Marguerite Higgins, and Joseph B. Harsch among others. But by the time he retired, his generation was giving way to a different kind of journalism, just as the management of newspapers was passing to the managerial, or business, professional. Today, in fact, so-called "print journalism" is being threatened by the revolution of the electronics and computer industries, which in turn is creating giant multimedia corporations. RBJ would have deplored the consequences of this situation.

With chain-owned newspapers in most cities looking more and more alike, as though stamped from some giant corporate cookie cutter, many no longer play the vibrant role they did when there were more of them and they answered to more different kinds of owners....The 'old guys' were independent newspaper publishers, many of whom were from families with close ties to their communities. In the 1980's Gannett's purchase of such respected papers as *The Des Moines Register* and *The Courier-Journal* of Louisville, KY., sparked heated discussions about whether news and corporate ownership could coexist.[154]

The question might be posed as to why the Church would attempt to attract to a top managerial position someone from outside the circle of talent that had been developed from within the organization, especially when many of that circle were descendants of the leading pioneer families of Utah. The climate of the times must be considered. In spite of the troubled relationship between the Church and the federal government late in 19th century, and regardless of the generally negative opinions of President Roosevelt and the New Deal held by many Mormons in Utah (including RBJ), Utahans were a patriotic bunch. When the war came, their instinctive patriotism - cultivated since the travails over statehood - prevailed. [155] Utah supported its President in the war effort and many Utah families voluntarily sent their sons, and not infrequently their daughters, to war. The fact that RBJ could bring to them, first-hand, the reality of what their servicemen were experiencing, would capture their attention. With his own penchant for the dramatic, and his genuine admiration for both the generals (and admirals) and the "doughboy," RBJ was a made-to-order local attraction. His popular appeal, of course, could also presumably be translated into greater advertising and circulation revenues.

Reflecting this desire, in fact, the news story announcing RBJ's appointment promoted his wartime career,: "Deseret News Officials Name War Correspondent As New Managing Editor: Ralph B. Jordan, Former Salt Laker, Saw Action In Pacific War Theater." The caption under the front page photograph of RBJ in his war correspondent's uniform read: "He saw General MacArthur in Action. Ralph B. Jordan, now managing editor of The Deseret News, was a war correspondent in the South Pacific, became intimately acquainted with General Douglas MacArthur and his staff in Australia and New Guinea." The history of the *Deseret News* reported it thus: "The News brought the war even closer to its readers by installing a battle-bathed managing editor. He was chubby, graying Ralph B. Jordan, fresh from serving as overseas correspondent for International News Service...Jordan's newspaper career had begun when, as a blond, porky boy of about fourteen, he had started serving as News correspondent for Salt Lake's West High School."[156]

Another "outsider," Merlo Pusey, Associate Editor of the *Washington Post* editorial page and who had been with the paper since 1928, had been offered the editorship of the *News* in 1939. So looking outside Utah for a Mormon journalist to edit the *News* was not entirely an aberration. However, Pusey elected not to return to Utah. He wrote: "Though flattered and pleased, I replied that I thought I could do more good in Washington, the best city in the world for journalism. Before leaving, President McKay gave me the impression that he agreed with that view."[157] Pusey did not feel that he had been "called," but rather that he had been "felt out." RBJ might well have regarded his employment by the Church as a "calling"; that would explain why he changed his career plans so abruptly and went with the *Deseret News* rather than remaining at MGM, when he had to leave the war zone for reasons of health.

Looking outside Utah for another newspaper was quite another matter. In 1915, J. Reuben Clark - a prominent Mormon attorney at the State Department in Washington, D.C., and later a member of the First Presidency of the Church - had suggested that the Church might become a silent purchaser of the *Washington Post,* which at that time was for sale. His justification was: "In my view nothing would be more advantageous for our people than the control of the policy of the Post in a manner friendly to our people. The good that such a paper could do us is beyond measure, it being located as it is here in the Capital and being read by practically every member of Congress." [158] The notion was not acted upon, but the episode illustrates how tempting it is for any religious organization to want to control a newspaper that can reflect its policies and beliefs before an influential public.[159]

RBJ would not have considered himself a "mouthpiece" for the Church, although obviously he had been a loyal executive for William Randolph Hearst and for Louis B. Mayer. His loyalty would have been based on secular rather than religious considerations. In this respect, he would have conformed to the following: "The true innovator will most often be a new person who has joined the organization but has not yet invested in it. He is one who most likely has not built his reputation based on the old rules. Moreover, his relationships within the organization are not such that he feels compelled to support the conventional wisdom...."[160] A former *News* colleague observed, years later: "Politically Ralph had to ride the rail in both his column and in coverage of stories. The *News* had a reputation of being biased toward the GOP and yet we were trying, circulation-wise, to wean over the so-called New Dealers. Ralph did this rail riding expertly, trying to gain friends on both sides, which he did. Ralph was too smart on most stories and in his speeches to offend and yet he never withheld his opinion.[161]

Although RBJ was no admirer of Roosevelt and probably never voted a Democratic ticket, he tried to bring a more balanced political tone to the news side of the operation partly because, according to Mary, he did not visualize his tenure at the *News* as the culmination of his career. Rather than the Church, the Utah political hierarchy, or the local community, he received his "psychic satisfaction" as a newspaperman from his journalistic peers. It probably did not surprise those persons who knew him well that he opted to return to that journalistic world, forsaking the security and local fame that remaining with the *News* would have continued to bring to him and to his family. Those journalists and columnists were never far from his mind, or his conversation.

Furthermore, to have cast him exclusively as an unknown and lonely "outsider" when he went to the *News* would have been wildly inaccurate, as this entire book reveals. He had grown up in Utah, had achieved a measure of local fame at an early age, and had mingled with contemporaries whose lineages, in Utah terms, were among the "top drawer." When he returned to Utah at the *Deseret News*, the city and state were full of people who either had known him or had known about him, and most, undoubtedly, wished him well. As he observed in one of his columns:

> This piece is addressed to and written for those harassed and gallant Mothers who watch their young offspring, the little male sprigs in their household, and wonder what in the world they will grow up to become. Their hearts are heavy and their patience sorely tried, but this is to tell them not to worry. Those little urchins, who seem possessed of genius for dodging their chores and annoying their elders, will grow up all right. You Mothers just stay in there and keep pitching, to borrow my own son's favorite expression, and those boys will wind up with a fine batting average in the game of life....

> Shortly after Dec. 7, 1941, the day of the Hawaii bombing, I arrived at Pearl Harbor as a war correspondent and heard, among other interesting tales, of a civilian who lived in a beautiful home in the hills back of Honolulu and who, that fateful day, had organized his neighbors into a well-armed squad and had taken his place with them to resist an invasion, to fight to the last for his family. I inquired as to his identity. He was a former assistant to the attorney general of the territory, a fine attorney serving important clients; serving them well and carving a reputation. Harold Kay was his name. What did he look like and where was he from? were my next queries.

He was described as blond, husky, good-looking and a former football player for the University of Utah.

In fancy I saw another day. I was writing sports for *The Deseret News* and was about to pick my all-conference grid team. Walking into the Sigma Chi house on the University campus, the first man I saw was Kay, which reminded me to not only put him on my squad but to name him the best back in the league, which I did and which he was. Several long Sunday afternoon walks in the Honolulu hills with Kay were among my most pleasant experiences in Hawaii. I think he's still there, although Mrs. Kay, a former Honolulu girl, daughter of a noted family in Hawaii, and their children now are in Ogden, his former home....

And speaking of bankers, it was only day before yesterday that I went into a Salt Lake bank to open a modest checking account and noticed a man who looked like Clark Gable and obviously was a very important cog in the organization. Employees were running to him and customers were tipping their hats. Now there, I thought, is the man I'd see were I here on big business. Then I looked twice. He was not only familiar, he was one of my best friends of campus days. Wendell Smoot is the name, another boy who really made good, and in his hometown. That's doing it the hard way.

In a West Coast navy yard a few weeks ago I was talking to the commandant when I heard his secretary, on the phone, say, 'Captain Ihrig picked it up yesterday.' I don't know what Captain

Ihrig had picked up, but I certainly knew Captain Ihrig, who went from East High to Annapolis and from a heroic ensign in the other war, with a navy cross for rescuing the crew of a torpedoed merchantman, to a captain in this war with a record as a skipper that will make a thrilling book, if and when it can be written. I know some of the chapters and planned on filling in the missing ones in the navy yard, but Captain Ihrig had slipped out to sea with his great ship the night before and was en route to bring discomfort to the enemy. Good hunting, Russ, you deserve it!

Near the University was a friendly home. Ihrig and I and the son of the house, Heber, would pick up a pal, usually Sandy Snyder or Grant Malmquist, and stage loud and rough boxing matches in the basement. It was the Sevy home… Bill Goodrich merely was one of the crowd on the football and basketball teams at high and the U, but he was returning to the United States as one of the famous mining engineers of South America when I last saw him in Oakland, Calif.

And then there was the phone call the other day here in my office in *The Deseret News.* The speaker identified himself as Marion Nelson, inviting me to lunch. Well, the last time I had lunch with Marion, I believe, was in a local high school cafeteria when we wished we had a nickel between us so we could split another meat pie, such items being but a nickel in those dear departed days. I'd heard from time to time that Marion was doing right well in the advertising business, but I didn't know how well until I made inquiry after his phone call. He's only the head of one of the best-known agencies in this part of the country. So, as I started out to say, don't despair, Mothers. You're raising the next generation of legal lights, famous commanders, noted engineers or advertising executives, no matter how they look to you now. Just be careful they don't become newspapermen.[162]

Undoubtedly, RBJ gradually became less - rather than more - convinced of the viability of his vision of what the *News* could become. In fairness, however, one must always keep in mind that the overall mission of the Church is to convert and to retain "souls," and its various commercial endeavors are regarded as means to this end. Everything that the Mormon Church does is filtered through the prism: will it protect the Church's reputation, retain the testimonies of its members, or enhance the missionary effort?

The Church leadership understood - or came to understand - the nature of RBJ's career in journalism, public relations, and publicity. They must have become convinced that bringing in RBJ would help enhance the *News'* journalistic prestige and change the character of its readership, still very rural-based, politically conservative, and Mormon *vis-a-vis* the more urban, politically liberal, and non-Mormon readership of the *Salt Lake Tribune* and the less-highly-regarded afternoon paper, the *Salt Lake Telegram,* both owned at the time by the Kearns family.[163]

The rivalry of the Mormon Church with the Kearns family stretched back to the turn of the century when there arose hostility between Senator Thomas Kearns and the Church. The newspapers had earlier in the century engaged in a vituperative relationship, and even today the **Tribune** is generally thought of as being self-consciously non-Mormon and, from the viewpoint of church partisans, as at times anti-Mormon. The *News,* in contrast, throughout most of its existence, has been viewed as an organ of the Mormon Church first, and a commercial newspaper publishing enterprise second.[164]

RBJ visualized turning the *Deseret News* into the leading newspaper of the Intermountain West, thus rivaling the *Denver Post* as well as the *Salt Lake Tribune*. This idea was probably too expansive because the Denver metropolitan area was so much larger and influential financially than was the Salt Lake area. Perhaps to compensate for this, he wanted to create a network of papers around the leadership of the *News* that would include the *Provo Herald,* the *Ogden Standard-Examiner,* the *Pocatello Post*, the *Logan Herald-Journal*, and other papers in neighboring communities.[165] To do so, however, would not only have been expensive; it would also have required, for example, more newsprint than was available: "The *News* had more than manpower shortages to contend with. An old ghost also returned. It was a paper famine....Beginning November 15, 1943 the size of the Monday paper was reduced to twelve pages. Thereafter there was a reduction in the size of other editions."[166] Financial considerations, especially the costs of newsprint on the one hand, and advertising revenue on the other, were, of course, always in the forefront of considerations for those persons responsible for any newspaper, and the *News* was no exception.

Shortage of newsprint was perhaps an even more acute problem for the *Salt Lake Tribune* because by mid-1943, the circulation had doubled to 80,000 daily and to almost 120,000 Sunday under publisher John F. Fitzpatrick. It, too, was forced into an arbitrary reduction in circulation and rationing of advertising.[167] Wartime inflation increased the costs of production, including salaries, resulting in severe financial constraints on both newspapers. Obviously, this situation limited whatever plans RBJ may have brought with him to enhance the *News'* position *vis-a-vis* its competitors. To put it bluntly, that RBJ must have had very little scope for initiative, and "holding the fort" until the problematic end of these conditions would have held little appeal for him.

In the late 1940s, conditions got worse as the *News* and the *Tribune-Telegram* found themselves engaged in a vigorous circulation and advertising war which the *News*, with its strong financial backing from the Church, was winning. The *News* could lower its circulation and advertising rates, thus undercutting the combined circulation and advertising rates of the *Tribune-Telegram*. Both owners knew that they had to find a way out of this situation, so the Newspaper Agency Corporation (NAC) was born. As it was described: "Massive losses by the *Deseret News* and disappearing profits, with prospects of insupportable losses, for the *Tribune* had at long last brought about discussion between the managements of the newspapers of possible solutions....The plan involved the sale of the *Telegram* to the *Deseret News* for merger into a single afternoon newspaper...and the transfer of business operations of the surviving *Tribune* and *Deseret News* to a non-profit, jointly-owned agency corporation,"[168]

Lacking this business-like arrangement, how could the circulation "playing field" be leveled between the rival Salt Lake City newspapers? One way was to rely on the use of "celebrity" to add some human interest, if not wartime credibility, to the *News*. To increase readership interest, RBJ signed on some of the most popular cartoon strips, and syndicated columnists.[169] This move, of course, increased expenses. The June 26th issue of the *News* used a full page to announce the new features: 'WE MEANT WHAT WE SAID...WHEN WE PROMISED YOU A BIGGER, BETTER DESERET NEWS!' There were eleven new comic strips (including two of my favorites - "Abbie 'n Slats" and "The Captain and the Kids"). The new INS writers were: Bob Considine - sports; Louella Parsons - Hollywood; Merryle Ruckeyser - financial; Richard Tregaskis, Clark Lee, Inez Robb and Pierre Huss - news; Norma Jean Wright - movies. RBJ also added Elaine Cannon as society editor and Edna Foster as women's editor. David A. Robinson became editor.[170] With these additions, the *News* was entering into a phase that placed it on a par in news and features with its competitor, the *Tribune*.

RBJ also got out and around the community, and would report on his trips and experiences in an informal and chatty way in his column, "Newsman's Notes." His column became very popular. It helped improve circulation and gave him a direct connection with the readership.[171] In announcing the column, RBJ was given a celebrity build-up:

> Announcing.... a new Deseret News Feature. Have you ever met General Douglas MacArthur, the No. 1 hero of the war to date for the United States? Probably not, but you'll have a chance, through a column in The Deseret News. And it will have practically the same effect and impact as a meeting with the noble warrior face to face; almost as good as a couple of hours' conversation with him...
>
> This...will be brought to you by Ralph B. Jordan, nationally famous reporter, editor and war correspondent, now managing editor of *The Deseret News*. He will write a daily column for this paper, starting next Monday, and his subjects will range widely, from General MacArthur, with whose staff he served in the South Pacific, to the latest from Hollywood, interspersed by what's going on in Salt Lake. You won't want to miss one of his articles.[172]

Additionally, in his first weeks as Managing Editor, he spoke to the Sons of the Utah Pioneers, the Salt Lake Kiwanis Club, the Antelope Island Chapter of the Footprinters Association, and the Salt Lake Exchange Club, among others. Marion C. Nelson, as President of the Salt Lake Rotary Club, invited him as a guest of honor at the Club's July 1943 luncheon. RBJ reported on the luncheon in his column: "...I noticed to my right a place card inscribed, 'King Clawson,' while to my left was a simple, dignified card reading 'Queen.' Considerably puzzled, I waited to see who would occupy the 'king' and 'queen' chairs, and what it was all about. The 'king' arrived first only it was a mistake...I mean, he wasn't a king...that's just his name...King Clawson...except it's really Kingsley Clawson...and he used to be known as Kink, but somewhere along the line the Kink got converted to King. Nobody can tell me much about Mr. Clawson for we were quite close a few seasons back...quite a few. We ran together...literally... on the same football team, at West High."[173]

He also spoke to a special assembly at Utah State, and to the Logan Lions Club. The Club's meeting was held in the Bluebird Cafe, which, coincidentally, was owned by Mary's relatives, the Cardons.[174] Stimulated by his visit to the university, RBJ made these comments about higher education:

> There isn't a finer school of its kind in the country, nor a more able college president [E.G. Peterson], but I wonder if the people of Utah fully appreciate them. If they do, they are a people apart for nothing is more difficult than to properly evaluate that which is close to us. One modest faculty member admitted Utah State is a pretty good cow college, which came as somewhat of a shock to me. The day of the cow college is gone forever, and gone a long time ago. Many of those students are studying agriculture, but their interest in the so-called cultural courses is undiminished. They want English, foreign languages, music, art and the various sciences, and they are getting them at Utah State and they should have them in abundance. Fact is, the cultural side of their educations should be stressed even more. It can't be stressed enough. The State of Utah should see that all the facilities to accomplish this are provided willingly and gratefully, for the combination of culture and technical training will provide the

real backbone of this nation, our finest and most charming citizens.[175]

RBJ sided strongly with University of Utah President, LeRoy E. Cowles, in support of strengthening the medical school, particularly in elevating it into a four-year program.[176] He felt that talented students should not have to leave Utah for good training. He would cite a statistic of Dr. Alan Gregg of the Rockefeller Foundation that only forty-two per cent of Utah students who left Utah for their medical education returned.[177]

Prominent political and civic leaders, such as the non-Mormon Mayor of Price (and later Governor), J. Bracken Lee, wanted RBJ to perform a public role in the community that transcended his religious affiliation or employment. RBJ reciprocated Lee's support, doubtless irritating the Democrats and possibly some Church leaders as well:

> Speaking of Mayor Lee reminds me of a conversation I had with a stranger yesterday at a service station on south State Street on the outskirts of Salt Lake where I was having a tire repaired. The stranger, just to make conversation, inquired my business and this led to mention of people we both know around the state. Finally Price came up and I said I knew Bracken Lee. Said the stranger: "Yes, I know him, too. He has done a nice job as mayor, but he's stubborn." I asked, "How?" and the stranger said: "Well, if he thinks he's right, there is no changing him. He's made a lot of people mad by refusing to do what they want." I made no comment, but thought that if that is an indictment, I'd be proud to have the same thing said about me.[178]

RBJ also spoke well of Salt Lake City Mayor, Ab Jenkins: "...he astonished me by his frankness...by the manner in which he discussed his experience while running for office and since he became mayor. He certainly beats about no bushes when he speaks of his opponents. He serves them up piping hot."[179] About Governor Herbert B. Maw he said: "The Governor is a man of rare personal charm...a convincing conversationalist...a most attractive personality. Were I opposed to him politically, I'd leave his doors and windows open so HE'D CATCH COLD AND COULDN'T TALK [*sic*]."[180]

He participated in a weekly radio show on KDYL, "Ask Your Senator," which featured, from Washington, Senator Elbert D. Thomas.

The Deseret News

Salt Lake City, Utah,   Friday, April 21, 1944

News Editor Takes New York Position

Ralph B. Jordan To Join Executive Staff Of International News

By Theron Liddle

Interviewing Senator Elbert D. Thomas

TAKES NEW POST—Ralph B. Jordan, Deseret News managing editor, accepts executive position with International News Service.

Resignation from the *Desert News*, April 1944

RBJ to INS; with Senator Elbert D. Thomas

99

At the time Thomas was Chairman of the Senate Foreign Relations Committee and a leading Roosevelt New Deal Democrat. RBJ would ask questions and the Senator would respond.[181] This made for a strange combination politically, because RBJ never relinquished his negative feelings about Roosevelt; in 1940 he had voted for the Socialist candidate, Norman Thomas, as a protest against both Roosevelt and the Republican candidate, Wendell Wilkie. As previously mentioned, his politics were fully in line with the conservative, anti-New Deal editorial stance of the *News*. In fact: "There were some cries that the *Deseret News* had become a voice of the Republican Party."[182]

For whatever reason (or reasons), when the call came for him to return to his first love – investigative journalism – this time in the guise of senior management as Assistant to the Editor-in-Chief of International News Service in New York City – RBJ doubtless jumped at the chance. Although this meant moving his family to a part of the country which was virtually unknown territory for them, the so-called "East" was not going to be unfamiliar for long!

Chapter Six

LIFE AND TIMES IN SCARSDALE: 1943-1945

"To outward appearances, Scarsdale belongs to the twentieth century. Yet among these gleaming white houses, these landscaped grounds and trees and winding roads, stand memorials of the past that have survived since the first decades of the eighteenth."[183]

A Unique Community

RBJ had sold his Pontiac coupe so the family drove across the country together in Mary's seven-passenger Buick Limited. They arrived in New York City full of enthusiasm for the new life that lay ahead. On his part, RBJ was to become the Executive Assistant to Barry Faris, the Editor-in-Chief of INS, which added to the excitement.[184] His offices were in the Hearst Building, located at 235 East 45th Street in mid-town Manhattan. Clearly, RBJ was reaching for the top of his profession, and it had been quite a climb from the newsboy's life in Salt Lake City before World War I, to international wire service executive in New York in the 1940s. Furthermore, unexpectedly, RBJ found himself in familiar company, because a very high percentage of the corporate executives who populated New York's affluent commuter suburbs had their personal origins in small cities or semi-rural communities similar to those of RBJ and Mary.

RBJ and Mary looked for a furnished rental house in the better inner suburbs, starting first in Forest Hills in Queens, which no one in the family liked, and then deciding on one in Scarsdale, in Westchester County. The village of Scarsdale nestles between the cities of Mount Vernon to the south, and White Plains to the north, with the towns of Rye and Larchmont on the east and Ardsley to the west. The Bronx River runs through the village, paralleled by the forested Bronx River Parkway, one of the earliest of this road network built. RBJ had heard of Scarsdale because that is where his boss Barry Faris lived. As it turned out, RBJ had rented a nicely furnished English mock-Tudor house at 154 Brite Avenue in the Greenacres section, just two doors from Faris - RBJ obviously was no shrinking violet!

He, along with his neighbors, commuted to Grand Central Station from the Hartsdale station, which was nearest to Greenacres, on the Harlem line of the New York Central. Next door to the Jordans were the Sigurd Larmons - he was a senior executive with the public relations firm of Young and Rubicam, so he shared something in common with RBJ. Larmon was a close friend of Dwight Eisenhower and played a leading role in Ike's obtaining the Republican Presidential nomination. RBJ felt right at home in this overwhelmingly Republican environment.

He found the house through the Midgley-Parks real estate firm - Lucille Midgley was from a Utah Mormon background. This is a small example of how those other members of the small Mormon community in Scarsdale, -or anywhere, for that matter - although similar professionally to their non-Mormon neighbors, nonetheless saw themselves as separate. Members of the "Mormon diaspora" – of which the Jordans had become leading members - looked out for one another as they climbed their respective ladders of success.

On the whole, the home was nicely furnished, especially for a rental house. There was a baby grand piano in the living room, which Mary Ellen played, plus a couch and stuffed chairs that were covered in the summer with a bright floral pattern, and comfortable wicker furniture in the adjacent sun room. Heating costs must have been high, or heating oil was scarce, because Mary was very frugal about heat in the house. In fact, she closed off the kitchen and maid's room and bath area on the ground floor for most of each day, and also the living room/sun room when she was not at home. So, for what would prove to be a brief time, RBJ and Mary, with the three children still at home – Mary Ellen, Bill and Bob - lived in a house as spacious and comfortable as that on Van Ness Avenue in Los Angeles, but in a much more private woodsy and upscale setting. In contrast, the Scarsdale home and surroundings were everything the rented house on Fifth South in Salt Lake City wasn't.

Scarsdale was and is one of the most affluent commuter communities in the country. Its beginnings can be traced to colonial times, but its growth as a sylvan suburb began prior to World War I. By the 1930s Scarsdale had emerged as a model of a London commuter village - the so-called "stockbroker belt" - complete with a central shopping area filled with mock-Tudor stone and brick buildings and railroad station. As early as 1915: "While some property holders...may have enjoyed the advantage of a large inheritance, they included few representatives of the idle rich."[185] There was a very high level of citizen volunteer involvement in carrying on the affairs of the Village. In fact: "Scarsdale is known throughout New York State for its efficient civic housekeeping, its high-grade schools, its freedom from political controversy through nonpartisan elections, its pioneer work in enacting a zoning law, and its generous contributions to charitable and philanthropic causes, in which churches and organizations join. This reputation was not attained without effort; behind it stands over fifty years of watchfulness and unselfish work by individuals who gave their time freely to benefit the community. The Scarsdale spirit reflects willingness to experiment, tenacity in carrying out aims and free play for individual opinion."[186] For example, all residents were entitled to join the Town Club, the main policy-debating body of the Village. Most of the business of the Village was ventilated through the Club's meetings, but the Scarsdale Women's Club and the churches were also places of public discussion.[187]

Scarsdale excelled in public education. It was said that its schools - along with its children - were Scarsdale's greatest asset, and that they compared favorably to such places as the school systems of Winnetka, Illinois, and Beverly Hills, California. The citizens expected: "...private school results from the public school system."[188] The aim was to prepare the students for entry into the best colleges and universities – a diasporan Mormon goal - and in this endeavor there is no doubt that it was successful. Another indicator of the quality was the strength of its administrators. For example, the principal of the high school from 1933 to 1953, Lester W. Nelson, was on the board of trustees of the Educational Testing Service, was an officer in the Middle States Association of Colleges and Secondary Schools, and had honorary degrees from Colgate University, Colby College, and the University of Pennsylvania.[189]

Mary Ellen, already mirroring her father, wrote for the school newspaper, the *Maroon*. She wrote a news and notes column called "Quoth the Jub-Jub Bird" taken from Alice in Wonderland. The yearbook was called *The Jabberwocky*. Like her mother later on when Mary was Southern California correspondent for the society page of the *Deseret News*, Mary Ellen brought in friends' names as much as possible. Here is an extract from one of her columns:

Dear Santa Claus:

I'm a little late this year with my letter, but I have a very good excuse. You see, we moved since last year to the beautiful town of Scarsdale and I've been kind of busy here - the teachers give more homework and they don't let you out as soon for Christmas vacation. ...I'm going to report on the kids in Scarsdale. On the whole, they're really a nice group of kids, and I want you to be generous with them. Of course, they have their moments. Now, take Ike Stewart for example. Underneath, he's a very sweet boy, but he makes me very angry every time he gets a better grade on a Chem. test than I do. You see, he stands up and yells across the room "What did you get? I got a 90." It always embarrasses me so to have everyone know I only got 40, or so.... [190]

The streets of Scarsdale, in keeping with the rural village atmosphere, were not lined with sidewalks, so people walked in the streets, slowing down car traffic. The Jordan children walked to school except in inclement weather, when Mary would get out the big Buick and cruise along Brite Avenue, turning the corner at Huntington Avenue to Brewster Road, then on Brewster through Fox Meadow to the high school, picking up other students along the way. Later, in the 1970's Bob's daughters Sara and Becky attended Scarsdale High School, with the younger Bob at the Junior High and David at the Fox Meadow School. Thus Bob's family had the advantage of being near the Westchester Ward building located just across the street from the High School and around the corner from their home at 40 Crane Road, in the Fox Meadow section.

Bob took a liking to school politics at Scarsdale and was elected to the student council where he became chairman of the Constitution Committee, an important committee at the time because it was charged with rewriting the constitution. Bill did well academically; he developed a reputation in the family as being the brainier of "the twins."

Bill and Bob were fascinated with Heywood Alexander, who was a member of an old and prominent New York family. The Alexander's small estate on Cooper Road in the Heathcote section included a large and rambling house, and a paddle tennis court - it could accommodate servants living permanently on the premises as could the Jordan's house on Van Ness Avenue in Los Angeles, from which they had only recently left behind. Heywood had gone to prep school most of his life but for high school his parents wanted him to try the public school, so the family chauffeur would drive Heywood to the door of the high school in a Lincoln Continental coupe in the morning and pick him up in similar fashion at the end of the day. This was their first experience with "old" wealth and what they came later to understand as the Eastern Establishment - a far cry from the *nouveau riches* of Southern California, or the professionalized Mormons of Los Angeles and Salt Lake City.

There were several Mormon families living in Scarsdale with whom RBJ and Mary became very close. These were June and Isaac (Ike) Stewart, a vice president of the Union Carbide Corporation; Donnette and G. Stanley McAllister, who had been an executive with CBS, and then was a vice president of Lord and Taylor Department Store (and at whose home the Jordans first watched television); and Nevada and Gordon Owen, who was with CBS. They all had children who were attending Scarsdale High. The Westchester Branch of the Church met in the Odd Fellows' Hall in Mount Vernon; Isaac Stewart was the Branch President. To illustrate how these Scarsdale Mormon families interacted, on the occasion when Bob was ordained a priest by his father, Branch President Stewart wrote to him:

> To hand you herewith your Certificate of Ordination to the office of Priest in the Holy Priesthood is, indeed, a privilege. As was so beautifully expressed in your Father's prayer ordaining you to that office, your advancement and achievements are a result of your faithfulness, diligence and proper living. Your participation in the activities of the Westchester Branch, in a willing, whole-hearted and efficient manner, has substantially contributed to the success of our organization. Our prayer is that you will continue

to bless Church organizations wherever you may go by your presence and contribution of time and talents. As an inspiration and beacon light, you have the ideal, exemplary lives of your Father and Mary. Your sister and brothers and you are patterning your lives from them. If you continue to follow your Father's and Mary's examples, true joy and happiness shall ever be yours, not only in mortality, but in eternity as well.[191]

To some, this language may appear excessive. However, it did reflect the Mormon linguistic style and the pride that all of those Mormons who lived in Scarsdale *ipso facto* shared - not only in their own achievements but also in those of their fellow Mormons. For example, in general, how many bishops or branch presidents in the church take the trouble to write such a letter on their personal stationery after each Aaronic Priesthood ordination performed in their unit?

Bob was the family member most active in the community affairs. A student/parent committee had been organized to create a youth center for the Village, and he was one of the student members. After much searching, the committee settled on an unused bowling alley that was in the basement of the Harwood Building, one of the main buildings facing on Boniface Circle in the Village center. With volunteer help, the place was repainted and fixed up, and given the name of "The Hanger." The whole enterprise received a lot of attention in the *Scarsdale Inquirer*.

As to truly public affairs, the Student Federalist branch of the World Federalist movement, which promoted Atlantic Union, also interested Bob. The inspiration came from Clarence K. Streit, the author of the widely-read pamphlet, *Union Now With Britain*.[192] The notion was that after the war, the democracies of Europe and the United States should evolve into a cooperative constitutional arrangement similar to the American federal system, thus moving away from fratricidal nationalistic warfare. The local student chapter was led by Harris Wofford, in whose Fox Meadow home it met.[193] Later, in the mid-1960s, it was revealed that the Student Federalists had been secretly - and unknowingly - receiving Cold War subventions from the CIA! Cord Meyer, Jr., one of the student founders, later worked for the CIA in promoting its cultural war against communism and the Soviet Union.[194] Perhaps there was an ideological justification, given the fact that the Communist dictatorships were anathema to the liberal democracies, but the entire effort was soon discredited as a violation of legal constraints on the activities of the CIA and inappropriate to a free society.[195] All such funding activities were banned. In a related political episode, Stanley McAllister served on the Board of Education from 1946 to 1951, which embraced the stormy period of Senator Joseph McCarthy's anti-communist attacks on educators.[196]

In summary, Scarsdale was indeed a unique community. House for house, there were more sumptuous residences in other Westchester County communities, and in terms of income, certainly other communities could lay claim to being at least competitive. What gave Scarsdale its distinctiveness was a combination of its own perception as a community and the civic-mindedness, strict zoning, outstanding schools, and obviously talented residents which provided a measure to which other communities around the country might strive. A backhanded way of putting it, made in the socially turbulent counter-culture of the 1960s, was that: "You have to grow up in Scarsdale to know how bad things really are." Put another way: "...whenever there is a strong sense of community identity, the members of that community must have some means of determining who belongs and who does not....in Logan, Utah, it is religion, and in Scarsdale, New York, it is social class."[197] RBJ and Mary had become a blend of both communities, and their children were their legacies. As this book reveals, they were as much a part of the "popular culture" of the times as they were of the "peculiar" culture of their religious heritage.[198]

154 Brite Avenue RBJ house

40 Crane Road RSJ house

Harwood Bldg., Boniface Circle with WW II memorial

Born To Fight

Return to the Pacific and Its Family Consequences

RBJ's family life took a turn for the worse when Joseph V. Connolly, RBJ's patron, died unexpectedly. The idea that he would succeed Barry Faris at INS was now dead in the water. Instead, RBJ was assigned by Faris to return to the Pacific as INS's Chief Correspondent, stationed in Honolulu. His instructions in December 1944 were: "With the Pacific and Southwest commands moving together so closely we have decided, for the sake of better overall coverage and the best possible disposition of our forces to place Mr. Ralph B. Jordan in complete charge of all our men in the Pacific.....I have asked Mr. Jordan to get out your way as soon as conditions permit to go over with you our set-up there and help you in every way possible to get the best organization going...."[199]

So RBJ left home and family again, and they were not to see him for nearly a year. Nonetheless, this was not an unattractive assignment for RBJ, given his personality and professional experience; but the second wartime separation from his family and the disappointment of not achieving that for which he had gone to New York, combined to add even more pressure to working under already stressful wartime conditions. In any event, some months later, RBJ suffered a massive heart attack and was hospitalized for eight weeks in a Navy hospital in Honolulu. During his initial recovery period he occupied a little bungalow on the beach. His friends on the *Honolulu Advertiser* and the *Honolulu Star-Bulletin* provided some companionship, as did several of Mary's relatives. On her part, Mary had been left on her own with three adolescent children in a part of the country which was not her natural Western-oriented habitat.[200] So she took a job with the *Reader's Digest* in nearby Pleasantville, which meant that when the children left for school in the mornings, she would take the train north.[201]

RBJ's heart attack changed everything. When Mary met him at the train station at Harrison upon his return to New

York, she was shocked to see him. He had lost a great deal of weight - yet he was still a large man with florid features - so that his clothes hung loosely on him. It was obvious that he had suffered a major and permanent health setback; and soon after his arrival home, to make matters worse, his gall bladder was removed at the White Plains Hospital.[202] He received some solace and satisfaction, however, when at the end of the war, General MacArthur sent him the following letter: "It is a real pleasure to me to award you the Asiatic-Pacific Service Ribbon in view of your long and meritorious service in the Southwest Pacific Area with the forces of this command. You have added luster to the difficult, dangerous and arduous profession of War Correspondent."[203] He also received commendations from Secretary of the Navy James Forrestal, and from Secretary of the Army Robert Patterson. The War Department awarded him an overseas theater ribbon.

Although RBJ's career at INS – and as a newsman - was finished, Hearst's King Features Syndicate asked him to write a book on Admiral William "Bull" Halsey, a hero in the Pacific war. So he wrote *Born To Fight* in the sun room, thus becoming unexpectedly a stay-at-home author![204] The book is still occasionally cited and quoted.[205] It falls into that class of military biography that found its parallel in the "booster" hyper-patriotic war movies of World War II. Obviously, the publisher was reaching out to that reading audience which enjoyed stories of heroism and glory, not reflective analysis based on careful historical scholarship.[206] In this important respect, they had a known quantity, for RBJ's anecdotal style of reporting lent itself to writing a generally admiring story of one of the war's greatest naval commanders. The book, in fact, is similar to Aimee Semple McPherson's *In the Service of the King*. They both were written in a breathless, fast-moving, highly personalized, anecdotal style. There is a partisan - even a defensive - tone to both books, as if the reader had to be persuaded that the subjects were indeed what they were claimed to be.

The claim concerning Halsey was pretty big: "...the boy who had gone away Bill Halsey, and come home Admiral William

Frederick Halsey, one of history's immortals."[207] In this passage RBJ appears to be giving a friend a boost: "Many people did not interpret the word 'victory' properly, as most strikingly told at the expense of a red-haired editor who fought at Guam. This young fellow, with the common name of Paul Smith and the uncommon faculty of making headlines instead of writing them, was a dynamic, carrot-top refugee from a collar ad who was editing the *San Francisco Examiner* before hostilities set in.... [he] went loping ashore on several Pacific islands at the head of his platoon, winding up in the initial waves of the leathernecks at Guam."[208] Whatever the merits of the book, having RBJ at home virtually full-time was a new experience for the family.

An important family event while RBJ and Mary lived in Scarsdale was Burdette's graduation from the Naval Supply Corps School at Wellesley College in Massachusetts. He had entered the V-12 officer commissioning program while at USC. The anxious competitiveness and status-consciousness generally felt in American higher education attached likewise to the numerous wartime military training programs. Getting admitted to and risking 'washing-out' of the various officer-training schemes was very like ... [doing the same in the civilian world]. Likewise, there were similar subtle social distinctions: the Navy V-12 program seemed the equivalent of Ivy, while going to Fort Sill, Fort Benning, or Fort Belvoir for ground-force officer training was like attending a state university.[209] They excitedly took the train up to Boston for the event - hailed as the first time boys were graduated from this famous girls' college!

Burdette visited the family in Scarsdale before he joined the Oakland Naval Supply Depot on the West Coast. In Oakland, he was shocked one day while working at his desk to look up and see an admiral standing there. The man was Rear Admiral Murray L. Royer, Inspector-General of the U.S. Naval Supply Corps, a close friend of RBJ's, who wanted to meet his son.[210] Fred was serving at sea in the Pacific, on the battleship *Pennsylvania* – fortunately, he survived its being torpedoed at Okinawa. Even though neither

Burdette nor Fred ever actually lived in Scarsdale, their names are inscribed on the World War II memorial in Boniface Circle in the Village Center. The policy was: "...every member of the armed forces with a Scarsdale home address, regardless of whether the family residence actually stood inside the Village, should be eligible for inclusion, if he or she desired."[211]

On the whole, the Scarsdale experience was an eye-opener to the family as a whole. Not only did they come to understand RBJ's career better, but the three adolescent children still at home also interacted more with both of their parents than ever before. They got a sense of the kind of life that RBJ and Mary had been living – juxtaposing the upward climb of RBJ's career with the domestic challenges that this brought to Mary. Although, as pointed out, both RBJ and Mary had been constantly urging all of their children to set high career goals as well as personal standards, it took Scarsdale to show how it could be done and with what result.

Chapter Seven

SOUTHERN CALIFORNIA, WHERE IT ALL BEGAN: 1945-1953

"Any fulfillment of the individual life cycle...can
only fulfill what is given in the order of things by
remaining responsible and by contributing continuous
solutions to the ongoing cycle of generations."[212]

Return to Metro-Goldwyn-Mayer and Life in Playa del Rey

In the summer of 1945, one thing was clear: RBJ's health and career
had been compromised at the time when his family's financial
needs were greatest. Mary Ellen had just graduated from Scarsdale
High School and had gone west to the University of Utah, where
she pledged Pi Beta Phi sorority. This unfamiliar intermingling of
church, secular, and family relationships imposed a severe strain
on her, which Mary Ellen resolved by transferring to UCLA,
a more comfortable social environment in which church and
family connections did not loom so large. "The twins" were still
at home and were entering their junior years in high school. At
war's end, Burdette and Fred entered graduate school, studying
law and medicine, respectively. Although they had the G.I. Bill to
help them, they could not be entirely self-sufficient, especially as

Fred and Betty also began their family. As a result, the financial challenges for RBJ as the family provider were at their peak.

Consequently, after he had completed his book on Halsey for King Features Syndicate, he decided to return to motion picture publicity. So the family returned to Southern California, where RBJ became Assistant to the Director of Publicity at MGM. This time RBJ was more closely involved in the overall work of the Publicity Department. Having known most of the executives and stars at the studio, and already well-known in the Hollywood community, RBJ was able to resume his responsibilities there fairly easily, although the change undoubtedly took a toll on his professional self-esteem. His career had plateaued, even though he had a good title and made a good salary.[213]

At MGM Commissary

RBJ with Ronald Coleman

The end of the war had changed the motion picture industry in several important ways. No longer was it pure entertainment. The experience of one of RBJ's *Deseret News* colleagues tells only part of the story of the nature of the industry:

> Suppose a tall dark man with a long black coat tapped you on the shoulder and offered to escort you through the biggest movie studio in the world. Would you go? Well I would, and I did, and here's exactly what the experience feels like. From outside, the MGM studio looks just like you'd expect it to look from movies you've seen of the gates, the walls and all that. Inside you're amazed at the size. Your first impression is that it's sort of a city made up of square white stucco buildings with no windows, and quite narrow paved streets.
>
> You see people walking about singly and in pairs. Some wear costumes. You notice a soldier with a torn

uniform, a pretty girl in a long filmy dress. You turn to your guide and say... "show me everything and point out everybody," and he says he will. A horn honks and you get out of the way of a swank roadster. "That's Bonita Granville," your guide says...," She's making a picture with Mickey Rooney on stage 8."

You're first impression is that a sound stage isn't a stage at all. It looks like an empty athletic field house. It's a big square building and from the ceiling hang countless ropes, scaffolds and scenes of all kinds. Standing everywhere on the floor are parts of bedrooms, of elaborate libraries with oil paintings on the walls. On the floor are cables, wires and rubber ropes snaking everywhere....You... enter a third set where Wallace Beery is acting. This is an unusual scene and you stand on first one foot and then another waiting for the men to get everything exactly right. You're amazed how many people seem to be doing nothing at all... just sitting. You count 39 men and six women - electricians, carpenters, directors, make-up men and actors.[214]

The industry had come to realize that it could have a profound influence on public opinion, having done so much to shape that opinion during the war. In fact, Hollywood had become a defense industry: "With Hollywood helping to shoulder the wartime burden of maintaining morale, there were few films that dealt with the reality rather than the romance of combat, or with the psychological effects of the war."[215]

Another change was that the movie-going public's tastes were not the same as before the war. Educators were complaining that the public was being treated by the moviemakers as if they were pre-adolescents, and that they were reluctant to show "realistic" films of American social life. Movie-going had declined from 85,000,000 to 55,000,000 by 1941 and this trend was likely continuing. After the war, the pollster George Gallup: "...described the typical movie fan as being 27 years of age, earning $28 a week, and strongly averse to patronizing pictures which dealt with the causes or probable consequences of the war. His or her favorite actor was Mickey Rooney. 'Mature' films were what was wanted."[216] If this seems like a contradiction, it is.

RBJ had written honestly and graphically about the horrors as well as the heroics and glories of war, and he felt that films should not hesitate to show both dimensions of the human experience. For RBJ, no movie exemplified war better than *The Best Years of Our Lives*, which he predicted would win an Academy Award in 1946. It was the top box office attraction in 1947. He would have agreed wholeheartedly with the appraisal: "It showed Americans as they are, presented their problems as they themselves see them, and provided only such solutions -- partial, temporary, personal -- as they themselves would accept. The picture's values are the values of the people in it."[217] These were the values of self-reliance, hard work, familial loyalty - the traditional values - that RBJ believed in. He would have agreed heartily with this comment: "...the era of human character which *The Best Years* makes available to its audience is a landmark in the fog of escapism, meretricious violence and the gimmick plot attitude of the usual movie."[218]

By rejoining his former associates in public relations and publicity, he and Mary knew that he was leaving reporting, his first love, for the last time. RBJ was, first and foremost, a newsman: a versatile writer and reporter who lived up to the INS slogan: "get it first, but first get it right!" Motion picture public relations operated according to a different credo which for him did not arouse the same kind of dedication and loyalty. MGM's motto was: "Make it good...make it big...give it class!" As it was put: "MGM was at its zenith between the late Twenties and the late Forties."[219] These were the years RBJ was involved - working either near, with, or for the studio.

They rented a house at 307 Fowling Street, in Playa del Rey, which is on the bluffs overlooking the ocean south of Venice and north of Redondo Beach and Palos Verdes; they would live there for the next two and a half years, enjoying, as it were, the sun and sand. The location was very convenient for RBJ to drive to the MGM studios in Culver City, and the fresh sea air and sun were good for his heart condition. He bought a Ford convertible which only he drove, presumably for his health! In those days, rest was about all that was prescribed for heart disease.

Playa del Rey house

Westport Beach Club

Playa del Rey was a residential community that had been planned in the 1920s, had lain dormant during the Depression years, and was just becoming revitalized. The prevailing architecture was Spanish-stucco style, with walled courts and red tiled roofs. Their house was set on a sandy hill, overlooking to the north was Bologna Creek and Marina del Rey, then still wetlands, and to the west was the ocean. A walled-in front patio featured a fountain. Fortunately, their furniture fit well, and after the heinous disruptions of the war, the family was once again reunited. Mary Ellen was living at home again while attending UCLA, and Burdette occupied the ground floor apartment while attending law school. Fred and Betty were living in their own home nearby in the Westchester subdivision, not far from Inglewood.

Living in Playa del Rey meant enrolling in nearby El Segundo High School because Playa del Rey had no school system. This was yet another new cultural experience for the twins. The town was dominated by the El Segundo refinery of the Standard Oil Company of California, and in fact, the company gave the El Segundo schools a generous subsidy. The parents of the twins' classmates either worked for the refinery, or in shops and service establishments, relying on trade with the refinery workers and their families. Bill and Bob had gone from living in one of the wealthiest communities in the country, dominated at the time by corporate or financial and banking executives, to one of the few remaining "company towns." But they adjusted rapidly, entering into school life with their usual vigor.

Bill distinguished himself as a letterman on the El Segundo High water polo team, which was recognized as one of the best in the nation. Coach Urho Saari was the builder not only of a water polo team, but also of young men; his praise and leadership inspired Bill and others to find the best within themselves and give it back to the team. Some of Bill's teammates became so good that they competed in the 1952 Helsinki Olympics, led by their former coach. After Saari died on December 29, 1990 he was memorialized by surviving El Segundo members of the

Olympic team in a simple ceremony in Yosemite National Park in 1992. A willow branch was placed in the stream as his widow commented: "The willow will float down the stream and take root. It symbolizes the legacy of Urho Saari that has taken root and has touched the lives of countless people."[220]

Bill was also Business Manager for the yearbook, the *Golden Eagle*, and Bob was in charge of subscriptions and photographs. The tennis team became Bob's sport, and as usual, he most enjoyed his social studies classes, thereby replicating his Scarsdale High School days by participating in student government activities as chairman of the Constitution Committee and as a member of the student council. Through these activities, he became friends with the principal, William P. Schlechte, but unfortunately, he left to become Superintendent of the Vista School District. Bob's other community service activity was with the Kiwanis Key Club, of which he was a founding member. The advisor was the superintendent of the refinery.

In sum, El Segundo had accepted the twins, and they were able to fit in readily, most likely because the war created such a high turnover of people. The local families learned how to accept newcomers more readily than they might have earlier. In June, after graduating, they spent that summer, along with Burdette, working on the night shift at Northrup Aviation, located near Inglewood. Not only did they make some college money, but also the three brothers spent lots of time together at the beach. It was a time of post-war renewing of bonds, with the three younger children interacting with the two older ones, who in turn could share their wartime experiences with their father.

There was no formal community structure in Playa del Rey, but the social life revolved around the Westport Beach Club, located on the beach front. The Club had been built in the 1920s, and it was enjoying a renaissance after the war.[221] RBJ joined as a family, but he and Mary seldom used the facilities. Mary Ellen liked to swim and lie on the sand. Burdette and Bill came occasionally, but Bob played paddle tennis and swam as often as he could and enjoyed the dances on Friday nights, which brought out many of the youth as well as their parents.

Renewing Church Ties and Creating College Ties

Although they lived beyond the Ward boundaries, Ralph and Mary were very active in the Beverly Hills Ward, located in the Beverly Hills Women's Club building at 1700 Chevy Chase Drive, north of Sunset Boulevard. The pull of longstanding personal ties was simply too great for Mary and RBJ to find a ward congregation near where they lived. Many of their friends from the Wilshire Ward years had relocated into the Beverly Hills/Westwood area, several of whom had children who went on to UCLA, together with Mary Ellen, Bill and Bob. Furthermore, new friendships were formed with many people who were also connected with the movie industry.

Mary and RBJ also made periodic trips to the San Diego area and the Hotel Del Coronado to watch the horse races at Agua Caliente in Tijuana. Many of the movie community, especially the directors and producers, liked to "get away" to the races at Caliente and at Del Mar. RBJ described the Del Mar track as "the little jewel box of a strip with the Pacific rolling almost to its lawns..." Both of them apparently fancied this spectator sport, and RBJ always liked to be around horses. As he said: "I love horses, love to watch them run, because they are the very spirit of flaming courage..."[222] Fred and Bill inherited this love; Fred always had a horse when he was practicing medicine in the Yucaipa/Redlands area, and Bill enjoyed the horses at Heber on the Hatch family property there. Always an outdoorsman, RBJ also found pleasure in ocean fishing from the piers or casting from the beaches.[223]

When Bill and Bob entered UCLA, it was understood that they would join the same social fraternity, or they would join none. Given RBJ's identification with Sigma Chi, and the UCLA chapter's desire to pledge both of them, the choice was easy. The Delta Eta chapter had been formed only a few years earlier, so they were involved in a new chapter of a well-established national fraternity. In fact, they were the first twin legacies to be initiated into Delta Eta, and were even featured in the May-June 1948 issue of *The Magazine of Sigma Chi*. They were initiated on March 21, 1948, and RBJ came to the initiation banquet.

Bill and Bob were very much involved in the life of the fraternity, and Mary Ellen had her life in Pi Beta Phi sorority. Scholastically, Bill was preparing to be a pre-med major, a goal which he had fixed upon early in life. Bob, on the other hand, was assiduously avoiding making a commitment to law school, which was what Burdette and RBJ wanted him to pursue. Instead, he majored in Political Science with a Business Administration minor, with no inkling as to what the future would bring.

Beginnings and Endings

In 1948 Burdette married Kathleen Patricia ("Pat") Jones, the daughter of Dr. and Mrs. Evan M. Jones. She had been in the Gamma Phi Beta sorority at UCLA, before completing nursing school. She was delivery supervisor at St. John's hospital in Santa Monica, where incidentally, her father was on the staff. They were married in the Mormon Mesa (Arizona) Temple on June 7th, with a reception at the Jones' home in Beverly Hills. After living temporarily in an apartment near St. John's Hospital, they bought a house in Westchester not far from Fred and Betty. By then, Burdette was fast approaching the time for the bar exams and Pat was expecting their baby.

By December the family was preparing for another marriage. Mary Ellen had become engaged to Raymond L. Haight, Jr., a USC Kappa Alpha fraternity brother of Burdette's. Ray had also served in the Navy and after a short stint in law school, was studying for his master's degree in history, with plans to teach in high school. Their formal wedding took place on December 20th in the Beverly Hills Women's Club, where the Beverly Hills Ward was still meeting. Betty and Pat were among the bridesmaids.

Beverly Hills Women's Club

The Family at Mary Ellen's and Ray's wedding

This was the last public event that RBJ participated in before he unexpectedly suffered a massive stroke. For this reason, Mary Ellen's wedding pictures carry special importance.

On Christmas Day 1948, RBJ had arisen and was sitting in his customary chair in the living room reading the paper, when he became ill and fell over. He was helped back to his bed, and Mary called Dr. Jones. Mary Ellen and Ray appeared - returning from their honeymoon - prepared to celebrate Christmas with the family. But a new reality had set in - an awareness of both the continuity and the fragility of life. The diagnosis which Dr. Jones rendered was not encouraging: if RBJ survived, he would be permanently disabled, both mentally and physically. For the first time, the family came up against the real possibility of RBJ's death.[224]

Although he tried to return to work, his movements were obviously impaired. It was evident that his usefulness was limited. Nonetheless, MGM was very considerate with him, leaving it to RBJ to decide when he felt he could no longer continue. Within a few months, however, it became clear that his career was concluded at the early age of 52, and that Mary was faced with caring for a semi-invalid just when her children were beginning to live independent lives. RBJ was angry that his body had dealt him this ultimate insult; he resented and fought against his situation. It was a tragic and difficult time for both of them.

In March, they bought a small cozy two-bedroom house on Altavan Avenue in the Westchester subdivision not far from Fred and Burdette. The house had a small den and an enclosed back yard. Bill was encouraged to transfer to the University of Utah to complete his pre-med studies, and to continue to court Jane Hatch, the daughter of Dr. and Mrs. Floyd F. Hatch, whom he had known since attending the Stewart School in Salt Lake City. Eventually Bob, too, claimed his independence by moving into the Sigma Chi fraternity house.

From his freshman year, Bob was very active in the fraternity, serving in nearly all of the offices, culminating in being elected chapter president the second half of his senior year. After his graduation, Craig Nason, the Grand Praetor of the Western Province, wrote Bob: "Allow me to express my regret that the Harry Lee Martin Exemplar Award did not start this year because, believe me, if it did, you would have been judged 1950-51 Winner. Bob, you are an exemplar 'Sig', having brought added luster to the White Cross by proving worthy of the badge you wear."[225] RBJ would have been pleased with this commendation because he valued his own affiliation with Sigma Chi. For Bob, being a "legacy" of RBJ was a point of pride, as it was for so many similar Mormon boys of his generation.[226]

As is true for many persons who have suffered a disabling illness, RBJ was hesitant about looking up very many old friends or former professional colleagues, although when he did they were genuinely glad to see him and treated him with consideration. He did look forward to mail and visits from some. RBJ's skills as a raconteur, although impaired, were still considerable, and he so enjoyed telling a good story!

To keep RBJ focused and with something to do, Mary started to write a society column for the *California Intermountain News*, a popular monthly paper directed at the Mormon community. She drew her material from the various social activities in which her children were engaged - which probably enhanced their social desirability! Her articles, "In Southern California," were also carried in the Sunday society section of the *Deseret News*. In addition, she did some illustrated feature articles in the *News'* magazine section; she was quite proud of her byline: "By Mary S. Jordan." RBJ tried to write some articles for various publications, hopefully for compensation, but after 1950, his diminished faculties prevented him from achieving a sufficient level of competence, which must have been very frustrating to him. He was, however, a good advisor to and friendly critic of Mary and her work. They continued to take short trips, mostly to the races at Agua Caliente and to Palm Springs, but also to various lesser-known tourist sites, where RBJ would collect materials for his stories.

In spite of an active life at UCLA, Bob became disheartened by RBJ's increasing limitations. For consolation, he would listen to recordings of the Mormon Tabernacle Choir or would read the sermonettes of Richard L. Evans that accompanied the Choir broadcasts.[227] The following passage was especially comforting to him:

> As we walk haltingly through life, repeating its mistakes and learning its costly lessons, we may sometimes be led to wonder why it is not given us to know more than we know. It would seem reasonable to suppose that we could do better if we were granted greater perspective - if we had more intimate knowledge of what has gone before and what is yet to come, back beyond the reaches of our memory and forward beyond the penetration of our foresight. But such thoughts are dispelled when we contemplate what does frequently happen when knowledge without judgment and power without conscience are found in the hands of a man. Such thoughts dissolve themselves when we realize that even now we have pushed the frontiers of abstract learning and material advancement far beyond our spiritual and social progress and have thereby upset many delicate balances for which we are paying a price. In the light of such things, it is easy to understand that the plan designed by the Creator is the one best suited to the good of man. And it would seem to be the course of wisdom to seek no greater power or dominion than we can justify by the use we have made of the facts and forces which are already in our possession.[228]

Bill and Jane were married in the Salt Lake Temple on December 22, 1950, with RBJ and Mary attending, leaving Bob the only remaining single child. After graduating from Temple University Medical School and serving in the Air Force, Bill returned to Salt Lake City where he served with distinction on the Medical School faculty. Bob went on to the University of Utah and from there to Princeton University for graduate work. Then he attended Oxford University, where he took a second doctorate. Thereafter his career took him to various universities and colleges both in the United States and abroad.[229] One of the things which sustained RBJ between 1948 and the early 1950s was his pride in the achievements of his children.

As for Bob, at the time of his commissioning as an Air Force officer, on June 14, 1951, he was named a Distinguished Military Graduate. Because the Korean War was underway, he received his reserve commission in the Air Force before his diploma, and so he knew what was to follow. Having been in the Pacific, and being strongly anti-Communist, RBJ had mixed feelings about Bob's going into this war. However he was grateful that he was in the Air Force, which was the least life-threatening of the three Services.

Bob's final duty assignment was as Adjutant of the Headquarters Squadron of the 27th Air Division (Defense), located at Norton Air Force Base, San Bernardino, California. This put him within commuting distance of Yucaipa, so for the three remaining months of his active duty tour, he occupied the same building that housed Fred's medical office at 34828 W. Yucaipa Boulevard, and in which Mary and RBJ had a small apartment. Unfortunately, the focus was still on RBJ's now rapidly deteriorating condition. He was having small strokes that left him less and less able to cope, but did not totally incapacitate him. The burdens on those caring for him, especially Mary, were becoming greater.

To Bob's surprise, and to RBJ's pride and pleasure, he was awarded the Bronze Star Medal for his work overseas.[230] It was pinned on him at a Saturday parade ceremony at Norton on June

13, 1953 (two days after his 24th birthday) by the Commanding General, Brigadier General Donald Hutchinson. The citation read:

> First Lieutenant ROBERT S. JORDAN distinguished himself by meritorious service as Personnel Officer of the 19th Bombardment Group, Medium, Kadena Air Base, Ryukyus Islands, from 7 April 1952 to 4 [March] 1953. Lieutenant JORDAN served in a position which normally required an officer in grade of Lieutenant Colonel and one with much greater military experience and background.... He was constantly faced with the problem of procuring personnel who were in limited and many times in critical short supply throughout the Air Force. He accomplished this under difficult circumstances. He established a manpower accounting and utilization system which enabled the 19th Bombardment Group to realize maximum effectiveness from all personnel assigned and thus had a direct effect on the Group's successful combat operations against the enemy in North Korea. Through his tireless effort, exceptional skill and devotion to duty, Lieutenant JORDAN sustained the highest tradition of the service and reflected great credit upon himself, the Twentieth Air Force and the United States Air Force.[231]

RBJ was too sick to attend the ceremony, but he expressed to Bob his pride in his having served not only honorably, but also with distinction, in wartime. Finally as Bob was preparing to leave Yucaipa to go to Salt Lake City to attend the University of Utah, RBJ's steady series of small strokes left him unable to contend with basic bodily and mental functions. It was tragic to see such a vital, optimistic, and energetic man slowly deteriorate in this way. Since it was becoming obvious that death could not be far away, Bob delayed his departure. He considered it one of the great disappointments of his life to not share with his father the experiences that lay ahead.[232]

The End of a Full Life

RBJ died in Yucaipa on September 23, 1953, and after a private funeral service two days later at Emerson's Mortuary chapel in Yucaipa, he was buried in the Hillside Cemetery on Sunset Drive in Redlands, not far from Fred's home.[233]

Obituary, *Deseret News/Salt Lake Telegram*, 22 September 1953

RBJ obituary

Hillcrest Cemetery, Redlands

The *Deseret News* ran the following editorial, along with a lengthy front-page obituary:

> During his more than 30 years of newspaper, press service and publicity work Ralph Jordan traveled widely, met thousands of people and wrote literally millions of words on the panorama of life as it passed before his eyes. He was a crack reporter with the proverbial "nose for news," and he wrote with an ease and sparkle of expression which gave his copy the "human interest" touch so highly prized by editors and readers alike.
>
> Many older Utahns recall "Jock" Jordan as a star athlete at the old Salt Lake High School and at the University of Utah back before the First World War. A few will remember him as editor of a weekly paper at Bingham and as a reporter around town shortly after the war. But he became best known here in the early 1940s when he returned from covering the war in the Pacific to become managing editor of the *Deseret News* and write a daily feature, "Newsman's Notes." In between times he had worked as a feature writer and editor on several West Coast papers and for International News Service, covering major stories of all types for a nationwide reader audience.
>
> Ralph Jordan saw the seamy as well as the glamorous side of life, yet he never became cynical or lost his sense of true values. He was a man of high principle, honest and forthright, affable and generous, ever ready to extend encouragement and a helping hand to a fellow craftsman - struggling young cub and down-at-the-heel old-timer alike. On learning of his

death in California Monday after a long illness, hundreds of newsmen throughout the country will recall their association with Ralph Jordan, one of the best in the business - a good reporter, a good writer and a good friend.

His obituary appeared in the *Los Angeles Examiner* ("Ralph Jordan, Ex-Newsman, Dies"), the *Los Angeles Herald-Express* ("Ralph B. Jordan, Veteran L.A. Newspaperman, Dies"), the *San Francisco Examiner*, the *Salt Lake Tribune*, the *New York Times*, the *Redlands Facts*, *Hollywood Variety*, and the *Hollywood Citizen-News*.

Ruth Woolley Austin, who had known RBJ in Los Angeles, in Honolulu, and in Salt Lake City, probably best summed it all up: "Ralph had a great talent, and if you have a great talent you are not on ordinary person. We tend to judge them by our expectations and are disappointed when they don't react the way we want them to because they are different. In reading this memoir [*A Newsman Remembered*] of his life, his family life must have been hard for him because his interests lay in areas that are about as far away from family and church as one can get. So in a sense he was out there all alone, and it would have to be a special woman to live with that and to pick up the looseness of their personal life in order to maintain the continuity of the family."[234]

In the next generation, RBJ's oldest son and namesake, Ralph, Jr., died also at a relatively early age:

Ralph Burdette Jordan, Jr., with wife Patricia "Pat" circa 1958.
l-r, top: Claudia, Burdette, Kathleen. l-r bottom: Mary, Pat,
Paul (on lap), RBJ III "Jock"

Former county counsel dies of heart attack at 66

imes-Delta **Saturday, January 21, 1989**

Staff reports

BAKERSFIELD — Ralph Burdette Jordan Jr., 66, a former Tulare County Counsel, died Wednesday night of heart failure.

After leaving Visalia for Bakersfield in 1963, Jordan became Kern County Counsel and earned a reputation as one of the most powerful men in that county — a hard-hitting lawyer, and a staunch supporter of the public's right to scrutinize the government in action, the Bakersfield Californian reported in its Thursday editions.

"He was a heck of a nice guy — we always got along famously," said Cal Baldwin, who worked for Jordan, then succeeded him as Tulare County Counsel.

Baldwin recalled the days when Jordan ran a three-person department, when the boss often worked nights and Saturdays: "From an employee's standpoint, he was always interested in how things were going for us. He was a

first-rate attorney — he always was."

"You could rely on him," said former county supervisor Ray Longley. "He was no-nonsense, but also very amiable."

Another former supervisor, Don Hillman, remembered Jordan as "always playing it cool."

"Nothing got him disturbed. He was a real steadying influence on the board. But he was jovial," Hillman said. "When he smiled, his eyes almost closed."

Perhaps the high point of Jordan's career with Tulare County was his state Supreme Court victory in a case against the state Board of Equalization.

"He was always regarded as a very brilliant man," said said current County Counsel Lita Blatner.

Jordan was born in Los Angeles, and received his law degree from the University of

See **Jordan**/2C

RBJ, Jr. obituary

Mary's Life After RBJ

Mary preferred to spend her years as a widow living alone in Yucaipa, not far from Redlands' Hillcrest Cemetery. She died of pneumonia on December 28, 1980, while spending Christmas in Bakersfield with Burdette's family; after Christmas she developed bronchitis for which she was hospitalized, but the deterioration was too rapid to save her. She may have had a premonition of her demise, because after her death, as her children and grandchildren gathered at her apartment in Yucaipa for a final farewell, they found a list which she had left on the table before leaving to drive to Bakersfield, matching up names with possessions of hers she wanted her children to have - the list had not been completed, but that it was there was touching. Her funeral, in the Yucaipa Ward, was on December 31, and she was buried beside RBJ in Hillcrest Cemetery. Six months later, Fred died and was buried nearby. Bill died in Salt Lake City in 1992, and is buried in Heber, Utah; Mary Ellen passed away in 2009 in San Francisco and her ashes were spread over the ocean.

She was described: "Mary was a humorous person who never seemed to be 'down.' If she was, she would shove it away - 'leave it until tomorrow and concentrate on today.' Mary did what she had to do when she had to do it. Mary could make the people around her laugh - she could see the bright side of just about any situation, which is probably what made it possible for her to hold the family together during the tumultuous years of her marriage to Ralph."[235] Ruth Woolley Austin commented that she was in awe of a woman that had this "inner something" that gave her such an outlook on life.

RBJ and Mary

CONCLUDING OBSERVATIONS

"We make much of seasons...and of fleeting events."[236]

Introduction

A newsman remembered is, in his children's lives, also a father remembered. In what ways did RBJ's life affect his children? How did his life affect those who knew him best? From the foregoing narrative, it is obvious that their lives were full of new social and cultural challenges as they moved from one community to another tracking his career. His career was always a source of fascination and considerable pride, spanning as it did journalism, public relations, motion pictures, wartime reporting, and various writing and reporting activities that involved him with the famous and the infamous. The people with whom he associated, whether linked to the Mormon Church or to RBJ's career, were persons of considerable talents and accomplishments.[237] The range of his acquaintances was enormous.

RBJ was a classic "Type A" personality, and his children were classic overachievers. An observer of Mormon success-oriented personality traits has identified four factors that have contributed to executive success: Education [Mary and RBJ met at college; their children possessed a total of two doctorates of medicine (Fred and Bill), one law degree (Burdette), two doctorates of philosophy (Bob), and one master's degree (Mary Ellen)]; Missionary

<u>experience</u> [RBJ insisted that education and military commissions should come before missions, having in mind the military draft - World War II (Burdette and Fred in the Navy), and the Korean War (Bob in the Air Force), and Bill (Air Force medical officer and then Flight Surgeon); <u>Public speaking experience</u> [with the exception of Fred, they were all verbally articulate in their careers, following RBJ's very public example]; <u>Family environment</u> - particularly strong encouragement and high expectations of parents to achieve. The children all experienced this pressure to the extent that they at times resented it, even as consciously and unconsciously, they strove to fulfill expectations.[238]

The Diasporans

It is noteworthy that within two generations of the settlement of the Utah-Idaho region, there was a "diaspora" of the youth to seek careers outside of Utah.[239] Many went to California, but others went to such places of opportunity as Chicago, Boston, New York City, or Washington, D.C. They often attended professional schools, and especially for law and medicine, George Washington University in Washington, D.C.[240] By the 1920s, talented young men from Utah were being named Rhodes Scholars at Oxford University. Paul C. Kimball, for example, took an M.Litt. at Oxford in 1930, having passed his *viva voce* examination with two of England's most distinguished economists, Roy Harrod and John Maynard Keynes.[241]

Having had this motivation injected into their lives, RBJ and Mary sought to pass it likewise to their children, as did the other diasporans. They encouraged their children to behave in a way that would attract the interest of persons, whether in school or in church, who would provide positive examples.

Because of RBJ's constant paternal urgings, and his claim that his children were "special," they worked harder to develop their talents than they might have otherwise.[242] He always noted with interest their various accomplishments, and would point out to them the long-term significance of what they were achieving in their overall personal development, as well as their career prospects. He was definitely a career guidance counselor! Equally if not more important, he wanted them to know that he not only loved his children, but also that he respected them. Consequently, they were always proud to be in his presence, and doubtless showed it, which must have been pleasing to him.

Mary was the moral tutor; she never failed to encourage her children to stay active in the Church, and she put her efforts behind what she said. She did not leave it to others to look after her children. Perhaps unfairly, the children began to see this commitment on her part as intrusive rather than constructive, but they never rejected outright the standards that she instilled. One of these was a strong sense of family loyalty. She constantly preached to them the importance of sticking together: "If you can't rely on your family, then who can you rely on?" Sometimes at times her children didn't take this advice seriously enough, to her frustration.

RBJ and Mary were not subtle people; there was a directness of speech and demeanor about both of them. They were hardworking and aggressive, yet well-mannered and sensitive to the opinions of others. They watched for the opportunity (the "main chance"), and then they would move to take advantage of it. To put it in contemporary parlance, they maximized their opportunities as best they could.

Although he was not much interested in the "old continent" of Europe, he regarded Asia and the Pacific as the natural place for America to find its destiny. In foreign affairs, his views were not too different from those of J. Reuben Clark, with whom he was associated while with the *Deseret News*: "[Clark] fought for public morality. He fought against the welfare state. He fought for individualism. He believed in an America of innocence and righteousness; an America whose diplomacy would be fair, open, and disinterested; an America that would exert moral leadership in the world... "[243] Today this would be embraced by the term "American exceptionalism."

RBJ shared with Clark suspicions about the efficacy of the League of Nations and later the United Nations, but he would have disagreed with Clark about using *only* moral force to achieve America's goals. RBJ was a firm believer in military readiness and admired the military profession, even though he was, at heart, an isolationist. RBJ enjoyed being around politically or militarily important people, especially if there was an element of the dramatic or of the theatrical about them. RBJ loved to be where the "action" was - and this meant for him studying and writing first and foremost about people, with events providing the context.

Although the Jordans were not a literary family in the conventional sense, they were a highly literate family. Neither RBJ nor Mary graduated from college; their "higher" education derived from their personal inclinations, from RBJ's career, and from their Mormon Church surroundings. They were practical, rather than reflective, people - doing was more important than just thinking. In fact, none of their children have been intellectually inclined in the pure sense of the term; they have had curious and questioning natures that continually open up new vistas for analysis, but they have not been drawn to the "cloisters." Although Bob was educated in two leading research universities (Princeton and Oxford), the "donnish" life was not for him.

Retrospectively, RBJ and Mary's family became, in short, the quintessential upwardly-mobile American family, reflective of the changing Mormon and American cultures of the first half of the 20th century. Their children of the second generation of the Mormon "diaspora" have in large part retained the cultural and religious traditions of their parents, even as they have adapted to the secularism of their own times. As an historian of Mormonism, Jan Shipps, contended, there was a lengthy period of "transition" or "adjustment" between the end of "...pioneer Mormonism, lasting from the 1890s to the 1930s, and the Mormonism of the modern age."[244]

The difference between RBJ and Mary in terms of the Church was precisely that Mary's upbringing - spanning the official outlawing of polygamy - was of the Pioneer church, whereas RBJ, as a convert in the 1920s, was of the transition to the Modern Church. The primary difference between the two cultures was that in the earlier period, Mormons were linked to and identified with sustaining the "elect" group (the sacred) against a hostile external world of the "gentiles" (the secular). According to Shipp, in the modern period, when the primary defining difference between the Mormon culture and American culture - polygamy - was banned, the Church turned to instilling in its members an individual, rather than a group, code of behavior to draw the distinction between the inner world of Mormonism and the outer world of secularism. Hence, Mary's constant insistence on family loyalty and Mormon Church activity.[245] RBJ looked at the Church as an outlet for service and as a means of bringing his marriage and his family together in the face of his otherwise highly mobile and secular family and professional existence. He stressed that each of his children should exercise his/her individual judgment in confronting life's problems, whereas Mary stressed that they should as much as possible derive solutions from Church teachings.

Their shared reliance for family sustenance and marital stability on associations with Mormons of their own career and educational backgrounds, derived from these two Mormon cultures. For Mary, it was an extension of the closed family life in which she was raised; for RBJ, it was the comfort of associating with people who had left that pioneer culture and were adapting to the highly individualistic culture that was shaping twentieth century America. As the sociologist David Reisman put it: "...with the virtually complete disappearance of tradition-direction, no possibility remains of learning the art of life in the primary group - a possibility that persisted even in the mobile families of the era dependent on inner-direction."[246] The Modern Church provided the inner-direction for the family, but they were not immune to the other-direction of the media-based "popular culture," which is why RBJ believed that motion pictures should be edifying entertainment and newspapers should be purveyors of real news and informed opinion as well as sensationalism.

Changing Leadership Styles

Put another way, two major leadership styles have been discerned in the Mormon Church: mobilization and articulation. "Leadership aimed at mobilization is leadership which emphasizes the exclusiveness of the movement, the absolute nature of its mission. Mobilization involves the reaffirmation of the movement's fundamental goals and values and is directed at building member commitment. The leadership of articulation attempts to link the movement and its goals to similar organizations and to the larger society. Emphasis on the uniqueness of the movement is softened, and greater tolerance for outside groups is promoted. Leadership which mobilizes is intransigent; leadership which articulates is conciliatory."[247]

During the period covered by this life story, the Church moved away from the mobilization and toward the articulation leadership style. It should be added, however, that one was not rejected in favor of the other; it has been more a shifting in emphasis and in attitude. No better example of this shift can be found than in the present President, Thomas Monson, who has been the embodiment of the articulation style during his entire career in top Church positions.[248]

RBJ and Mary were not hostile toward the "mobilization" style of identification as Mormons; instead they and their children could be described as uncomfortable being identified *only* in this way. As they moved about from one urban environment to another, and also moving socially up the rungs of the middle class ladder, the children tended to become more comfortable with the "articulation" style. They were more interested in stressing what they, as a family, shared in common with their friends and neighbors than what differentiated them. The nature of RBJ's career, as well as his personal beliefs, would underscore even more strongly this generalized family attitude.

RBJ would not have applied this observation about J. Reuben Clark to himself: "...once having beaten the East, Reuben found that he had also resolved his crisis of identity."[249] For Clark, this meant returning to Utah from a successful career in Washington, D.C. In contrast, RBJ had resolved his "crisis of identity" before he had returned to Utah - his identity was in pursuing the news-making lead story or lead personalities of the day, which meant being where the "action" was. If he had not had a failure in his health at a relatively early age, a convincing argument could be made that the Jordans would either have continued to live in New York or eventually in Southern California, for these were RBJ's familiar haunts. These were the places where this "popular culture" was being defined and disseminated to the nation and to the world. Settling down in the place from where he embarked on his career, and from where his marriage began, was not for him. To be lionized in Utah as a "native son" returned - as was Clark, and for a brief time as was RBJ - would not have satisfied either RBJ's temperament or his ambitions.[250]

Afterword

TWO PIONEER TRADITIONS

"...every man shall have his land measured out to him
which he must cultivate in order to keep it."[251]

Introduction

It is appropriate after reading of RBJ's and Mary's lives, to describe in general who their immediate forebears were, and what their respective families were like. Several observations must be made at the outset. They came from similar "stock," albeit RBJ's was predominantly German, and Mary's was predominantly English.[252] Both were descended from small farmers and artisans or shop workers who left their native villages in search of new opportunities in frontier America. For RBJ's German ancestors, this meant settling in the humid and forested frontier lands east of the Mississippi; for Mary's English and Welsh ancestors, it meant settling in the arid and desert-like West. Neither sets of emigrants were prepared for what lay ahead for them; they had to learn new skills, to endure unanticipated hardships, and to confront the insecurities brought on by hostile Indians. Both sets came from Protestant religious backgrounds, possessed strong religious convictions, and relied heavily on family ties for their succor.

Settling Along the National Road

RBJ's earliest known American pioneer forebear on his mother's side was Johann Melchior Hengerer, a ducal gamekeeper in the "old country"; he and his wife, Elizabeth, arrived in Philadelphia with their family on the ship *Robert and Alice* on December 3, 1740. In 1744 they settled in Lancaster County, Pennsylvania and became members of the Trinity Lutheran Church. Like many other immigrating Germans, the Hengerers had left villages of the Neckar Valley near Heidelberg in a region known as the Kraichgau. Records of them have been found in Hessgen, Neidenstein and Daisbach (among others), where Johann Melchior and Maria Elisabeth were married in 1723. In America they were part of the expanding migration of Germans in the 1740s into the Quaker colony of Pennsylvania.[253] As the movement was described: "... each year thousands of redemptioners from the Palatinate and southwestern Germany, with a mingling of Swiss Mennonites, came to the Quaker colony. By this time most of the land in the eastern section was either occupied or held at prices beyond the means of impoverished immigrants....The frontier, with its cheap land, was the region for settlement best suited to the necessities of the newcomers and most agreeable to the Quakers. Thus it was that the 'Pennsylvania Dutch' settlements were founded to the northward as far as the Lehigh and to the westward around Lancaster..."[254]

The Hengerers did not stay there long, for by 1751 Johann Melchior's sons, Johann Frederich and Peter, had purchased land in Greenbrier County, Virginia. They were lured there by land speculators because the large-scale migration of the previous decades to Philadelphia had driven up Pennsylvania land prices; from 1727 to 1754 at least fifty-thousand Germans had entered America through Philadelphia.[255] Virginia also had rich but affordable land, which the Hengerers and their German compatriots purchased from the huge land grants of men like Robert Beverley,

Benjamin Borden and Lord Fairfax. The Hengerers, in fact, did buy their lands from Beverley and Fairfax.

These settlers "... came on horse-back and their effects were brought on pack-horses... They were building houses and barns; opening roads; building mills and churches; and establishing schools to give their children at least a common school education."[256]The Hengerer brothers built their cabins near each other on the Greenbrier River, thus displaying a general tendency of the German settlers to maintain intact their family and kinship groups, even while they were settling on dispersed family farmsteads. They accomplished this by intermarrying, by speaking German, and by retaining their customs. But they also adapted rapidly to the economic and commercial environment in which they found themselves.[257] In fact, it has been observed that the German immigrants were better at farming than their English co-settlers.

The Hengerers/Hangers might have been either restless or entrepreneurial land speculators, for they left this part of Virginia ten years later, when they bought land in Woodstock, Shenandoah County. Frederich Hengerer donated land on November 6, 1764, for the Woodstock Lutheran congregation to: "Erect and Build a Church thereon and a school house if necessary" - known as Emmanuel's Church. [258] An altar cloth embroidered in German was donated by Eva and Frederick Hengerer. The embroidery translation was: "Friederich Hengerer, Eva Margareda Hengerin, Woodstock To God Alone the Glory 1767." Then in 1769 they sold the Woodstock property and bought more land in Augusta County, Virginia. Frederick bought 225 acres between Staunton and Middlebrook, and Peter, by then a saddler, bought 187 acres in Beverley Manor, near Staunton.

Just as the Hengerers were typical in moving within ten years from Pennsylvania southward to Virginia, they were also typical in the size of the holdings that they bought and farmed. Most of the Germans from southwestern Germany considered ten to twelve rented acres a substantial holding, thus, by averaging at first purchase in America 152 acres, the Hengerers very likely considered themselves large landowners.[259] Several of the Hengerers also took time out from their farming and other activities to fight with the colonials in the War for Independence.

Johann Frederich, who still wrote and spoke in German rather than in English, died in Augusta in 1799. He left behind thirteen children, presumably all by his wife, Eva (nee' Mayer), who was probably his cousin. He also had been a member of St. John's German Reformed and Lutheran Church, from whose records much of the knowledge of the Hengerers was obtained. By the early 1800s, his son, Charles/Carl (who was able to read and to write in German and English), had Anglicized the family name to Hanger, and had moved to Ross County, Ohio. This was a natural evolution, for many German settlers were moving westward at the time, following the migration trails that paralleled or intersected the great National Road, built after the Revolutionary War to facilitate the opening of the trans-Appalachian frontier. It was an upgrading and extension of the famous Cumberland Road. The Hangers most probably took the Kanawha Branch of the Great Indian Warpath to Chillicothe, the county seat of Ross County.[260]Again, they were not alone in their migration or in their possible motives.

Many who left New York and Pennsylvania were frontiersmen who, living on the western fringe of civilization, drifted naturally with the moving tide. In Virginia... soil exhaustion forced thousands to abandon their farms...Some of the democratic small farmers occupying the region went west to escape contact with slavery, others disliked the new class stratification which placed them on a lower level than the great planters, while still others were displaced when their lands were absorbed by plantations. Between 1790 and 1800 thirteen counties in Maryland and twenty-six in Virginia lost population, so rapid was the migration.[261]

RBJ's great-grandfather, Charles Hanger, Jr., was born in Springfield Township, Ross County, Ohio, on September 18, 1818. He married Sarah Jane Burgess in 1844, in West Liberty,

Logan County, Ohio, and owned land there, but perhaps did not move there permanently until after 1850; he is shown on the 1850 federal census as a resident of Harrison Township, Ross County, on land adjacent to his parents. Dunkard Hill Church of the Brethren Cemetery, also in Harrison Township, has a tombstone marking the grave of Susannah Hanger, Charles' Mary, and stating her death date as 1851. His father, Charles, Sr., or Charles/ Carl is also reported to have died in Ross County in 1854.

Until 1994, it was believed that RBJ's grandfather, Frederick Allen Hanger, was born at Mt. Tabor, Champaign County, Ohio, immediately south of Logan County.[262] His Civil War pension file, however, reveals that his birth was in Ross County, that he grew up in Champaign County, but that he enlisted for military service in Logan County; he was a drummer boy with Ohio's 66th Volunteer Infantry, Company K, and later with the 4th U.S. Artillery.

It is understandable why the Hangers were attracted to the region of Champaign and Logan counties: "West Liberty, centered in the midst of a rich grain and livestock district, drew the Mad River and Lake Erie railroad, which was completed in 1849, making West Liberty the shipping point of all grain and livestock in this part of the country."[263] Even today the area consists of rich farms that lie around the county seats of Urbana in Champaign County and Bellefontaine in Logan County. Many Hangers settled in this area in addition to RBJ's direct forebears, as the record of land sales and transfers for the years 1856 to 1883 testifies. Many members of the extended Hanger family, or the families into which they had married, were involved in land speculation as well as settlement.

In the early 1870s, the younger Charles sold his holdings in Ohio and followed two of his older brothers, John George and Frederick, to Clinton, De Witt County, Illinois. Charles ran a grocery/mercantile goods store there, remarried after the death of his wife in 1872, and died there in 1898. His son, Frederick Allen, became a butcher, and married Eudorah Kirkpatrick, of

Mt. Tabor, Ohio, on March 6, 1873. She was descended from a prominent New Jersey family; photographs in front of a photo-covered piano suggest that she may have had an awareness of culture and the "finer things of life." Five children were born to them in Clinton - Maud (who died before 1880), Myrtle Estelle, Theron Maximillian, Curtis, and Elmer Allen. By the 1890s, Frederick was running a boarding house in Chicago, where he and Eudorah were divorced on August 26, 1903; this apparently was the first divorce in either of my parents' families, perhaps a sign of the coming times.

Frederick Hanger - his photos show him with beautiful white hair, a twinkle in his eyes and a genial demeanor - immediately remarried, to Charlotte Lingenfelter, who was his partner at the boarding house, and they moved to Glendale, California, where he ran the Glendale Hotel at East Broadway and Glendale Avenue, for many years. Following the death of Charlotte in 1930, he married in 1933 a widow, Olive Ryckman, who was living at the hotel. He died on the twins' tenth birthday, June 11, 1939, in San Fernando, Los Angeles County. During much of his final decade, he lived in the Veterans Hospital in Sawtelle, West Los Angeles, where Mary visited him periodically while she lived in Los Angeles.   His son Elmer with his wife Caroline, lived near the Jordans; being childless, they more or less "adopted" nephew RBJ's family.

Settling the Valleys of "Zion"

Born on July 4, 1853, near Keokuk, Iowa, Mary's father Orson Gurney Smith was the eldest son and second child of Thomas X. Smith and Margaret Gurney.[264] The family were Mormon converts emigrating from Eton Bray, Bedfordshire, England, to Utah. The Smiths originated in the nearby larger town of Leighton Buzzard, from which Thomas X's grandfather moved to Eton Bray. Thomas X. Smith was a hatter by trade, and knew nothing about coping with a frontier lifestyle, nor did his wife.

Thomas and Margaret Smith, with their baby daughter, Lucy, sailed from Liverpool on the *Falcon* to New Orleans in 1853.[265] From there they traveled up the Mississippi River to St. Louis, and then overland to Omaha. Omaha was a major staging area for the Mormons to organize themselves into handcart companies or wagon trains in preparation for the journey westward across the Great Plains and the Rocky Mountains. The Smiths arrived in the Salt Lake Valley shortly before General Johnson's Army briefly occupied "Deseret."

They first settled in Farmington, just north of Salt Lake City, but two years later, in 1855, Brigham Young directed them to resettle in Cache Valley.[266] "The colonization of the Great Basin was not left to chance. The locations were determined by scouting parties, who traversed wide areas. The leaders chosen were called to that work by the authority of the Priesthood. They were carefully selected men. The founding of settlements became a religious duty to which families were called, in the same way that their sons were called to carry the Gospel into the world."[267]

Mary's family on her mother's side - the Wrights from Yorkshire, and the Gibbses from South Wales - came to Utah as Mormon converts in 1859, and also settled in Cache Valley.[268] John Pannel Wright had been a ship's captain, and because he knew how to plot locations by the stars, he was called upon to survey the first town plots in Cache Valley. The new town came to be known as Smithfield (for another settler). Later that year he surveyed the city of Logan. The year officially designated as the founding of Logan was 1859, the year Wright laid out the city. In 1860, the new community of rough log cabins was named Logan - also by Wright. The pattern of early settlement was described: "The first homes were dugouts on sunny slopes; single rooms that were perhaps fifteen feet square. A rock chimney stood at the side or back, bearskin and buffalo robes covered the hard-packed earth floor. With good fortune there was a door of logs - otherwise a heavy blanket might serve to close the entrance. The walls were whitewashed with lime applied on a sheep-skin swab."[269]

John Wright's founding role was reported: "Logan City was first settled by twenty-one families in May, 1859, the heads of said families being...John Wright. July 3 - Bishop Peter Maughan, at a public meeting, appointed John Wright, John Nelson and Israel J. Clark, a committee to give out the land. John Wright was appointed to receive tithing and forward the same to Maughan's Fort, and from there to Salt Lake City."[270] All of Mary's Mormon forebears were involved in the planning and construction of the Logan Temple. Orson Smith almost lost his life helping to set up a sawmill in one of the canyons to handle the logs being gathered for use in the temple construction.

Then, early in the 1860s, the Wrights moved south of Logan and helped to settle the town of Paradise.[271] John Pannell Wright's son, John Fish Wright, and his wife, Martha Duggan Gibbs, moved his family onto unsettled land at Old Paradise, later designated as Avon.[272] Their daughter, Mary Ellen Wright Smith, was born there on January 4, 1865. Martha's father, George Duggan Gibbs and his family also lived in Paradise. Not long after Mary Ellen's birth, John Fish Wright moved his family to farm land he owned, located between Hyrum and Paradise, which meant leaving the relative comforts of a frame house in Avon for a more primitive log cabin.[273] Here, he established a dairy herd and looked after his crops.

Orson Smith was called to be the Bishop of Paradise Ward at the age of twenty-two. At first he was not accepted by the congregation because he was thought to be too young and inexperienced, but the resistance eased when he appointed a counselor who was older. Of the first meeting of her father and Mary, Martha Smith Lee recounts: "When twelve years of age she first became acquainted with her future husband. He had been called from Logan to act as bishop of Paradise Ward and came there with his young wife [Caroline Carpenter]. He was getting out rock for a new meeting house and called at her father's house for his oxen. His first impressions of her were in his Sunday School class where she attracted him with her keen, bright mind and ever ready questions and answers."[274] Near the time when Orson became a member of the Cache Stake presidency in 1877, he took a second wife, Sarah Ann Obray, and moved to Logan and set up his two households there.[275]

John Pannell Wright was among the first to be called to form a High Priests Quorum.[276] Although he and his wife, Martha, were faithful and practicing Mormons, they were opposed to polygamy. So when Orson Smith took notice of their daughter and oldest child, they were not happy. Nonetheless, Orson and Mary Ellen were married - in secret - on July 4, 1884, in the Logan Temple, where plural marriages had just begun to be performed. Margaret Carpenter Smith observed: "We children knew nothing about the courtship or the marriage until one Sunday father brought her home with his other wives, and asked us how we'd like to have a new auntie. We were all very glad because we knew how much we loved our present auntie."[277] As one of his daughters - not from Mary's family - observed: "Mr. Smith's proposing was very simple and direct. He didn't do any extended courting; he just asked the girl if he might come to see her, and then soon, if she would marry him. We didn't have any marriage licenses in those days. When I, II, got married to him, we went to Salt Lake to the Endowment House. Yes, Carrie went along with us."[278]

Orson and his two wives, Caroline ("Carrie") Carpenter and Annie ("Auntie") Obray, lived on a farm. They had a hired hand to help run the farm, and Carrie taught school to earn money.[279] Orson also taught school. When he was home, he would spend "week about" with his wives, unless it was for a shorter time, when he "divided his days between them."[280] When they first moved to the farm in Paradise, each wife had her own bedroom, sharing the other rooms; when Orson built a larger house, each wife also had a sitting room.

Mary Ellen's own words describe how she came to believe in polygamy: "I graduated from the district schools and received a scholarship to the University of Utah. Father did not want me to go so I went to Logan for higher education. I attended the B.Y.C. They met in the basement of the tabernacle and later at the college. It was there I studied theology under J[ames] Z[ebulon] Stewart. He especially emphasized the marriage covenant with plural marriage as the most desirable. The first wife was as a good foundation while if you stopped there the main structure was never completed. This and many more he used as illustrations for that principle. I was converted. In reflecting back now there was a goodly number of that class impressed and went into it, boys and girls."[281]

With her marriage and almost immediate pregnancy, Mary Ellen had to live the life of a fugitive from the law because polygamy had been officially outlawed, although it was still tolerated by the Church. To her parents' credit, the Wrights helped to provide her refuge and succor.[282] She lived first with her parents but in 1886 went, secretly, to Cardston, Alberta, Canada.[283]

By the time her youngest daughter Mary was born on September 9, 1898, Orson was a leading citizen and Mormon Church leader in Logan, having been the President of the Cache Stake from August 2, 1890, to October 29, 1899. During Mary's childhood, the Smiths could be characterized as having been "of modest means but respectable," because of the financial uncertainties surrounding Orson Smith's activities after the turn of the century. She described her family and childhood as "poor but happy."[284] Her memories were captured in this description of their life:

Her father had taken three wives. They were taught not to do or say anything that would derogate Grandpa Smith's "patriarchal" standing as head of the family.

> They had a total of twenty-seven children. Mary's mother's family had ten children. Her father used to spend two weeks with each family in rotation. By the time Mary was born there was little left in

the way of ready cash. However, the spirit in the family was such that they would not have known what you meant if you had said they were poverty stricken. The older children frequently took in the younger ones after they were married both to help relieve the financial strain on the family and because they were used to having a crowd around and felt lonely.

The children did not lack for friends in their youth - there were plenty of relatives to play with. Also, they were always so busy that they had little time to become bored. The boys were responsible for the outside work which included the five cows, the farm behind Aunties' house [the second wife], the red barn in the 'gap,' and the vegetable garden. The girls were responsible for all of the housework. Those who learned to sew made the clothes for the others. Before they left the home, Aunt Nell did the washing and Aunt Martha did the ironing and mending. Aunt Olena subsequently became the most skilled seamstress.[285]

Her parents were devoted to each other and to the Church. As Mary reported: "Father and mother were very lovely to each other and showed their affection to the extent that we kids thought they were mushy at times..."[286] Their dedication was also evidenced not only by the church positions which they held over the years, but also by the fact that they continued to have children - some of whom were born in Canada - for over a decade after the Manifesto which declared that polygamy should cease. In the issue whether church or state ruled supreme, they were loyal to the teachings of their church, as were many others. So it was not entirely surprising that Mary Ellen Smith bore children in 1895 (Owen), 1897 (Olena), 1898 (Mary), 1901 (Seymour), 1903 (Walter), and 1904 (George), during which time his other surviving wife, "Auntie," also bore him children. With his three wives, Orson Smith sired nine children after 1893.[287] It may not be coincidental that he had his last two children (by both wives) in 1904, for: "The Manifesto marked the beginning of a radical shift in Mormon self-identification during which the Mormons remade themselves into archetypal Americans."[288] In 1904, in order to quell rumors that were threatening to unseat Utah's Senator Reed Smoot, church president Joseph F. Smith announced that any member of the Church who continued to practice polygamy would be excommunicated. It took President Heber J. Grant in 1910 to make this policy stick. The Mormon Church knows a lot about both obeying and disobeying secular authority.

The society was hierarchical and patriarchal. For example, Thomas X. Smith was Bishop of Logan Fourth Ward for forty years, which Mary said was the longest tenure of a bishop in the history of the Church. [289] He was one of four bishops at a time when the Ward organization was the dominant form of religious authority in the community. The fact that Thomas X. was also a justice of the peace did not vitiate this point, for initially "the justices of the peace were all Mormon bishops."[290] A framed portrait of him still hangs in the Ward meeting-house, and the Ward erected a monument over his grave in the Logan City Cemetery.

As to education, the children were sent to church day-schools for which tuition was charged. "Everything that was done was done with the purpose of making the whole family one single unit. There were many children and they were encouraged, in fact it was the rule, to find their pleasures at home. They were bought musical instruments and an instructor was brought in to teach them to play so that they had their own orchestra. They gave little plays and 'recitations.' All this was done in the home and apparently the audiences were just the family. There was a strong feeling of solidarity. Anyone seeing the family would have been unable to discriminate between the children of the different mothers."[291]

Orson penned this verse:

<u>Out West</u>

The great outdoors has gone, that once aroused the zest
In human heart and bone and moved them to the West.
No more the Indian trails traced on hill and mountain crest,
No more the bear and coyote wail is heard out in the West.
No more the fish and game abound for trapper and the rest.
No more is the silence found that once pervade the West.
No more the miles of waving grass, like carpets of the best,
On hill or dale where we pass; is no more seen out West.
The scene had changed apace, the wilderness gone to rest;
subdued by civil race, God Honored and God blest.[292]

Notes

1. Verlin Klinkenborg, "The Ideal Family Vanishes on Film,"- a review in *The New York Times*, January 29, 1995. Portions of this book are drawn from: Robert Smith Jordan, *A Diasporan Mormon's Life: Essays of Remembrance* (Bloomington, IN: New York, NY: iUniverse, rev. ed., 2009).

2. Myrtle Estelle had four brothers: Theron, Maximilian, Curtis, and Elmer Allen. Harry had a sister, Lavicia A. Jordan, born in September 1858, married to John A. Grey in October 1877; and F. Burdette Jordan, born in September 1863, and married to Emma A. Parsons in February 1886. Very little else is known about them and their families.

3. Mary claimed that he played baseball for Drake University, but the University has no surviving records that attest to this.

4. The 1900 Federal Census of Salt Lake City, Utah, shows them living in the Third Precinct. Listed with them is John Harris Jordan, Harry's father, who is buried in the Salt Lake cemetery. Research efforts have not uncovered where Harry's mother was in 1900, but she died in Salt Lake City four years later and her body was shipped to Des Moines, Iowa, for burial.

5. This issue also reported a story about the Salt Lake Newspaper League: the *Telegram* baseball team (on which RBJ played) decisively beat the *Tribune* but lost to the *News* team. The *Telegram* team claimed that the *News* team had some professional players on it.

6. See Joel E. Ricks, ed., *The History of a Valley: Cache Valley, Utah-Idaho* (Logan: Cache Valley Centennial Commission, 1956). In those days, football was everything in terms of intercollegiate sports - basketball was not yet a major sport, and baseball was not nearly as prestigious.

7. Sources and dates unknown. Clippings are from a family scrapbook.

8. *Deseret News*, January 19, 1943.

9. *Deseret News,* January 20, 1943.

10. See Afterword for Mary's family antecedents.

11. See William Jordan's history of Mary Wright Smith Jordan.

12. Another version is that Mary worked in the bookstore. Very likely she had several jobs during the approximately four years that she was on the campus.

13. *Deseret News*, February 6, 1943.

14. *Deseret News*, February 6, 1943.

15. "My Life."

16. Postscript to Mary Ellen Wright Smith's history.

17. Mary, in her history, described Madigan as being "silver-tongued."

18. Undated news clipping, "Newspaper Man is Athletic 'Boss' at University: Ralph Jordan Selected to Handle Business End of Teams at State 'U'" (source unknown).

19. William Jordan's history of Mary Wright Smith Jordan.

20. In her history, Mary says that she happened to be in Salt Lake City at the time (letter of March 25, 1993 to Mary Ellen Haight); William Jordan's history of Mary Wright Smith Jordan.

21. "My History."

22. "My Life."

23. Mary Ellen Wright Smith's history.

24. See "My Life."

25. Letter, George Gibbs Smith.

26. William Jordan's history of Mary Wright Smith Jordan.

27. It may not be entirely coincidental that for a short time in 1923, the Mormons in the Los Angeles area met for dances in an upstairs hall at Broadway and 54th Street, called the Rose Room. RBJ was a member of the YMMIA Stake Board at the time. (See Leo J. Muir, *A Century of Mormon Activities in California,* vols. 1 and 2 (Salt Lake City: Deseret News Press, 1952). Since the entries were written by the persons or families included, their accuracy could not be established.

28. Adela Rogers St. Johns, *The Honeycomb* (Garden City, N.Y.: Doubleday and Co., Inc., 1969), p. 56. She was the daughter of one of the most famous trial lawyers of the time, Earl Rogers, and she went on to become one of the leading woman reporters of *her* time - which coincided with RBJ's career.

29. *Deseret News*, May 19, 1943.

30. Recounted in the *Deseret News*, February 10, 1943. RBJ's general theme in this column was that persons who don't give luck some credit for their successes - who pose as "fountains of wisdom, as infallible oracles" - were irritating.

31. David Halberstam, *The Powers That Be* (New York: Alfred A. Knopf, 1979), p. 116

32. William Randolph Hearst was famous for personally choosing his editors - and also for firing them - which doubtless put more pressure on people like RBJ. As I was growing up, I recall RBJ talking about John B.T. "Jack" Campbell, the city editor of the old *Los Angeles Herald*, which Hearst had bought in 1913. Campbell must have been both a friend and a competitor.

33. St. Johns, p. 96. The houseboy was a suspect, as was Normand's mother.

34. For a description of the events and the trial, see Andy Edmonds, *Frame-up! The Untold Story of Roscoe "Fatty" Arbuckle* (New York: William Morrow and Co., Inc.1991).

35. Edward W. Knappman, ed., *Great American Trials* (Washington, D.C.: Gale Research Inc., 1994), pp. 294-299.

36. William Smith Jordan's history of Mary Wright Smith Jordan.

37. This is the house to which Bill and I were brought as newborns, as well. They had first lived in the Adams Ward of the Church, and then the Florence Ward.

38. For example, Fred's, Spanish-style house at 620 West Sunset Drive, in Redlands, had been the winter home of the White Truck Company family of Cleveland. It had orange groves around it, two servants' houses, a guest cottage (the Casa), tennis courts, and a three car garage. For more on this point, see Robert S. Jordan, *A Diasporan Mormon's Life: Essays of Remembrance* (New York: iUniverse, Inc., 2009).

39. John and Laree Caughey, *Los Angeles: Biography of a City* (Berkeley: University of California Press, 1976), p. 277.

40. Caughey, p. 279. A prominent family of Mormon pioneer lineage, Dr. William E. and Jean Cannon Hunter, lived in Fremont Park. Many of the prosperous Mormons discussed in this book sent their daughters either to Marlborough or

to the Westlake School for Girls, located in Holmby Hills, a wealthy residential area not far from Beverly Hills.

41. Larry May, *Screening Out the Past: The Birth of Mass Culture and the Motion Picture Industry* (New York: Oxford University Press, 1980), p. 190. The Mormons of RBJ's and Mary's generation were not immune to this attraction, as the following chapter shows.

42. Daniel Mark Epstein, *Sister Aimee: The Life of Aimee Semple McPherson* (New York: Harcourt Brace Jovanovich, Publishers, 1993), p. 315.

43. See Robert C. Tucker, "The Theory of Charismatic Leadership," *Daedalus* 47(Summer 1968).

44. Joel Tibbetts, *Women Who Were Called: A Study of the Contributions to American Christianity of Ann Lee, Jemima Wilkinson, Mary Baker Eddy and Aimee Semple McPherson*, doctoral dissertation, Vanderbilt University, May, 1976. For a general discussion of psychological attributes, see William J. Bouwsma, "Christian Adulthood," in Erik H. Erikson, ed., *Adulthood* (New York: W. W. Norton and Co., Inc., 1978), pp. 81-96.

45. Quoted in Kenneth Howard Shanks, "An Historical and Critical Study of the Preaching Career of Aimee Semple McPherson," doctoral dissertation, University of Southern California, 1960, p. 36. In this respect, it is interesting to compare her to the "ministries" of other American female evangelists. See, for example, Tibbetts, pp. 424-425. Of the four, Mrs. Eddy was the most obviously concerned about institutionalizing her ministry, although she insisted that her own role be the center of focus. Later in his career, RBJ aspired unsuccessfully to replicate the success of the *Christian Science Monitor* as a leading national church-owned newspaper by making the *Deseret News* a leading regional church-owned newspaper.

46. Shanks, pp. 88-89. At about the same time, according RBJ's father Harry joined the Angelus Temple congregation. It is not surprising that he was attracted to the Foursquare Gospel, for he was not untypical of her congregation as a whole. In contrast, Anthony Quinn the movie actor was introduced to the theatrical world through his peasant Mexican grandmother's conversion from Catholicism to the

Foursquare Church. In his autobiography, *The Original Sin: A Self-Portrait* (Boston: Little, Brown and Co., 1972), esp. pp. 122ff. Quinn captures the excitement that surrounded the events at Angelus Temple, and the compelling personality of Aimee. It is interesting to also note that in the 1995 movie "Forrest Gump," the hero mentions the Foursquare Gospel as one of the pillars of his upbringing in rural Alabama in the 1930s.

47.　Epstein, pp. 369ff. See also Arthur M. Schlesinger, Jr., *The Crisis of the Old Order: 1919-1933* (London: Heinemann, 1957), p. 213, esp. ch. xxiv. Schlesinger captures very effectively the mood of the times in which Aimee Semple McPherson flourished. Schlesinger quotes William Allen White: "Effective relief, said William Allen White in September 1931, would be 'the only way to keep down barricades in the streets this winter and the use of force which will brutalize labor and impregnate it with revolution in America for a generation'" (p. 178). For more on utopian thought, see Frank E. Manuel, ed., *Utopias and Utopian Thought* (Boston: Beacon Press, 1966).

48.　Epstein, p. 369. The Commissary opened in August, 1928.

49.　It is interesting to note that the videotape prepared by the Mormon Church on the life of President Gordon B. Hinckley when he assumed the Presidency in April 1995, displays some London newspapers of 1936 headlining one of Aimee's revival tours at the time that President Hinckley was a young missionary also preaching in London's Hyde Park.

50.　St. Johns, p. 87. Ralph Wheelwright went to MGM in 1930, where he became assistant publicity director until 1943. Thereafter he became a full-time screenwriter and also a producer. His most famous screenplay was "Blossoms in the Dust," for which he was nominated for an Academy Award for an original screen story. For a complete listing of Wheelwright's writing and producing activities, see John Douglas Eames, *The MGM Story: The Complete History of Fifty Roaring Years* (New York: Crown Publishers, Inc., 1976). RBJ joined Wheelwright at MGM a decade later (see also Ralph Wheelwright's obituary in the *Hollywood Variety*, April 19, 1971).

51. St. Johns, 1969, p. 86. St. Johns perceptively noted: "Nor could anyone overlook her political power, she did not separate church and state, she spoke out on radio to hundreds of thousands, to millions....Public opinion was split right down the middle about Aimee, half believed she was the most inspired evangelist since St. Paul, the other that she had to be a fraud and was a scandal to Christianity." (pp. 86-87).

52. Epstein, pp.252-253. He went on to observe: "This was the environment Aimee made her home in 1923. She would live and die across from Hollywood, in the twilight between fantasy and reality, in a love-hate relationship with the press" (p. 25).

53. See Ruthven, *The Wilson Quarterly.*

54. St. Johns, p. 87.

55. Lately Thomas, *The Vanishing Evangelist: The Aimee Semple McPherson Kidnaping Affair* (New York: The Viking Press, 1959), p. 317.

56. Epstein, p. 316. The reference to the attorneys probably includes former Utahn Roland Rich Woolley, who resigned when she would not conform to his legal advice.

57. Robert Bahr, *Least of All Saints: The Story of Aimee Semple McPherson* (New York: iUniverse, 2001), p.148.

58. Lately Thomas, *Storming Heaven: The Lives and Turmoils of Minnie Kennedy and Aimee Semple McPherson* (New York: William Morrow and Co., Inc., 1970), pp. 61-62.

59. Thomas, *Storming,* pp. 61-62.

60. Keyes quoted by Thomas, *Storming.*

61. Thomas, *Storming*, pp. 134-135.

62. Thomas, p. 134.

63. See Epstein. Aimee's mother's attorney was Arthur L. Veitch, who later was to be a neighbor of RBJ when the family lived on South Van Ness Avenue. Veitch was by then working in the District Attorney's office.

64. See Thomas, p. 318. Mrs. Wiseman even claimed that Woolley had "improper relations" with her when they attended the same high school in Salt Lake City. Her sister, Mrs. Virla Kimball and her mother, Mrs. Clara McDonald, supported her. Woolley had to prove that this was impossible (p. 318).

65. See Muir, entry for Roland Rich Woolley. It was observed: "As chief counsel, Woolley (a Mormon who was destined to hold positions of trust and esteem in his church)...." (Thomas, p. 120).

66. See, for example, Thomas, pp. 137ff. Ormsby had been retained as her legal counsel, but he was very much involved in financial matters. Because many of the rumors that swirled around RBJ likewise swirled around Ormsby - financial manipulations, ill-thought-out promotional projects, personal ties with Aimee - it might appear that, rather than being the shady manipulators several authors have suggested, they instead were knowingly and willingly "used" by Aimee to carry out activities which she desired but which would have been opposed by the regular church administrators and by her family.

67. Information on Cromwell Ormsby comes in part from Ralph B. Jordan III, who knew some of Ormsby's descendants in Visalia, California. On August 2, 1890, when Orson Smith became Cache Stake President, Oliver C. Ormsby was made Superintendent of the Stake Sunday School, and in 1899, Marietta Ormsby was Secretary-Treasurer of the Cache Stake Primary; they, presumably, would be the parents of Cromwell Ormsby, so it would be difficult not to draw the conclusion that RBJ and Cromwell Ormsby would have known - or known of - each other from a common association with Logan and Logan families (Curtis, pp. 19-21).

68. Epstein, p. 333. The most noted criminal lawyer of this period, Jerry Geisler, also worked for Aimee. He went on to do some legal work for RBJ, and even wrote a letter supporting Burdette's application to law school at USC. Geisler handled many of the criminal trials and divorce actions of the famous and infamous in and around Los Angeles during the 1920s and 1930s (see, for example, St. Johns, p. 357). See also "Geisler's Rise to Glory in L.A. Courts," *Los Angeles Times*, January 4, 1998.

69. Epstein, pp. 252-253. Aimee was also very thoughtful and generous.

70. Interview of Jane Jordan with Ruth Woolley Austin, October 26, 1995.

71. Aimee Semple McPherson, *In the Service of the King* (New York: Boni and Liveright, 1927), p. 218. Mary claimed that RBJ ghost-wrote this book. She also claimed that he wrote another book, *Two Black Aces*, but apparently there is no evidence that it was ever published. Robert V.P. Steele, writing under the pseudonym of Lately Thomas, noted that *In the Service of the King* was ghost-written, but does not say who the author was (see Thomas, *Storming*, p. 354). In his book, *The Vanishing Evangelist*, Thomas recounts an episode wherein Aimee had considered a ghostwritten book over her name to be written by one Oliver Allstrom, a free-lance writer. Nothing came of it, although the title *Kidnaped* was considered. (pp. 261-262). Boni and Liveright was founded in 1917, and initially thrived on the Modern Library, reprinting classics. It published, from 1920 to 1930, such notable literary figures as Bertrand Russell, Eugene O'Neill, Dorothy Parker, Anita Loos, S.J. Perelman, Hart Crane, and National West. (See Christopher Lehmann-Haupt, "The Disastrous Life of a Pioneer of Hype," *The New York Times*, July 27, 1995, p. B2).

72. Thomas, p. 95.

73. The deed to the lots was dated 1930, which probably means that it took this long for the affairs to be settled legally.

74. This episode brings to mind Evelyn Waugh's brilliant satire on the mores of the American undertaking business and of Hollywood, *The Loved One: An Anglo-American Tragedy* (Harmondsworth, U.K.: Penguin Books, 1948.)

75. This was, in fact, quite fitting, for Forest Lawn was full of celebrities: "[Jean Harlow] was twenty-six years old when she died. The love of her life was Bill Powell and it was Bill who bought the stately white marble tomb at Forest Lawn, where two million people a year go to see the Thorveldsen Christus, the reproduction of Michelangelo's *Moses*, and the window of *The Last Supper*, the finest stained glass in America." (St. Johns, p. 177.) . In 1944, at his mother's death, her son Rolf K. McPherson became president and chief minister of Angelus Temple. An obituary of Lorna McPherson, his wife, described the International Church of the Foursquare Gospel as including more than 600 congregations and a Bible College (*The New York Times*, June 18, 1993).

76. Leo J. Muir, *A Century of Mormon Activities in California,* vols. 1 and 2 (Salt Lake City: Deseret News Press, 1952), pp. 482-483.

77. This was the official slogan of International News Service (Information Brochure, undated). RBJ mentioned this MGM slogan frequently.

78. International News Service Press Release, March 10, 1930. The Pacific Coast Manager's territory included San Francisco, Los Angeles, Sacramento, San Diego, Portland, Denver, and Alaska. The official history of the 1930 Los Angeles Olympics lists RBJ as the news reporter covering the Games (see California Club Library). Mary felt that RBJ would have won the Pulitzer Prize for his reporting on the Point Honda naval disaster if he had not been working for Hearst, who was a bitter rival of Joseph Pulitzer.

79. W.A. Swanberg, *Citizen Hearst: A Biography of William Randolph Hearst* (New York: Charles Scribner's Sons, 1961), p. 301.

80. For more on this, see John K. Winkler, *William Randolph Hearst: A New Appraisal* (New York: Hastings House Publishers, 1955), pp. 279ff.

81. See John Tebbell, *The Life and Good Times of William Randolph Hearst* (New York: E.P. Dutton and Co., Inc., 1952), pp. 310ff.

82. Information brochure, *International News Service,* undated, but probably written about 1935.

83. Quoted by St. Johns from a letter to his publishers, October, 1928, p. 185.

84. INS brochure.

85. Later, competition came from the General News Bureau, controlled by Moe Annenberg. See Ferdinand Lundberg, *Imperial Hearst: A Social Biography* (New York: Equinox Cooperative Press, 1936), pp. 304ff. As Lundberg observed: "In the Hearst organization all the sports department men speak highly of him, while the news department men are bitter. The explanation lies in the perquisites that fall in the way of the sporting writer, who is not hindered in collaborating with sporting promoters... " (p. 304).

86. *Deseret News,* February 20, 1943.

87. In 1991 the Oakland-Berkeley hills burned, destroying more than 2,600 homes, but fortunately not theirs, because, apparently of the tile roof. The house is virtually the same as it was in the 1920s. As the area is described today: "It is hard to imagine a more bizarre construction site than this fire zone. A few streets into the hills, the vegetation suddenly stops. Gargantuan new houses crowd together on the naked hillside, testimony to the fire victims' desire to build as many square feet as the new zoning laws allow. Remains of dead trees and charred foundations make a surreal backdrop." (Diana Ketcham, "An Architect Conjures Up History From the Ashes," *The New York Times*, August 17, 1995, p. B1).

88. Chad M. Orton, *More Faith Than Fear: The Los Angeles Stake Story* (Salt Lake City: Bookcraft, 1987), p. 81.

89. Orton says the "Country Club" refers to the Los Angeles Country Club, but a glance at a map reveals that the Wilshire Country Club, near the Hancock Park section of the Wilshire District, is more likely the inspiration. Other sources for this chapter are the Hollywood Stake Manuscript History, and the Los Angeles State oral history collection. There is also G. Byron Done, "The Participation of the Latter-day Saints in the Community Life of Los Angeles," doctoral dissertation, University of Southern California, 1939.

90. See Muir.

91. Orton, p. 81. By the late 1930s, the Church began to draw away from the Hollywood image, dropping the name from the rosters of Stakes when a reorganization took place that year.

92. See Orton, Chs. 5 and 6, for a full description of the situation. Interestingly, President McCune had also, as he put it: "... [come] to Los Angeles under appointment to prepare for the organization of a stake of Zion in Los Angeles County" (Muir, vol. 2, p. 72). Previously he had served as President of the Eastern States Mission whose headquarters were in New York City. McCune came from a wealthy family; a relative, A.W. McCune, had been one of the leading mining millionaires in Utah. He had invested in real estate development in the Mar Vista area, near Ocean Park with Charles B. Stewart, Sr. and there is a street named after him, on which presumably he had built his home.

93. Orton, p. 103.

94. Orton, p. 104.

95. The name of the Stake was changed because the General Authorities had grown to dislike the association of "Hollywood" with the Church because of the "atmosphere of the movie industry," (Orton, p. 122).

96. This same attitude surfaced elsewhere, where there were concentrations of successful Mormons of the "out-migration." See, for example, Carri P. Jenkins, "Out Migration: Making Home Away From Home," *BYU Today*, May 1989, pp. 39-44. This article discusses the concentrations in Minneapolis, New York City, and Washington, D.C.

97. See Ralph Wheelwright's obituaries in the *Hollywood Reporter*, April 16, 1971, and *Hollywood Variety*, April 19, 1971.

98. For a readable history of MGM, see Gary Carey, *All the Stars in the Heaven: Louis B. Mayer's M-G-M* (New York: E.P. Dutton, 1981).

99. See Bernard Weinraub, "Hugh Grant's Arrest Seizes Hollywood," *The New York Times*, June 29, 1995, pp. B 1-2.

100. St. Johns, p. 160.

101. Carey, pp. 175-176. As was to be expected, RBJ had a special interest in that model of American masculinity, Clark Gable; he also knew and liked Judy Garland, who had her own set of personal and professional problems for people like RBJ to deal with.

102. Leo C. Rosten, *Hollywood: The Movie Colony, The Movie Makers* (New York: Harcourt, Brace and Co., 1941), p. 135. See also Greg Mitchell, *The Campaign of the Century* (New York: Random House, 1992).

103. A very good book on the subject of the movie industry and politics is Ronald Brownstein, *The Power and the Glitter: The Hollywood-Washington Connection* (New York: Pantheon Books, 1990). This was not the first political victory for Mayer involving Hearst. He was successful in persuading Hearst to support Herbert Hoover in the presidential election of 1928, thus endearing himself to the Hoover Republicans (for a discussion of the Hearst-Mayer relationship, see Carey, p. 114ff).

104. The earliest mention of a Mormon Haight apparently is Morton B. Haight, who was captain of a Mormon pioneer

company that included B.H. Roberts' mother, that crossed the plains in 1862. The Mormon branch also went on to California a generation later. Hector Haight was an attorney in Los Angeles and his daughter Elizabeth - "Liz" – went to UCLA, and David Haight was a businessman in Palo Alto and local Mormon leader before going to Salt Lake City as a General Authority.

105. He also resented being identified with press agents - or "flacks" - who hovered everywhere in Hollywood. There were, literally, hundreds of press agents trying to promote the careers of their clients, not all of whom had equal talents.

106. Robert W. Desmond, *Tides of War: World News Reporting, 1940-1945* (Iowa City: University of Iowa Press, 1984), p. 241.

107. *Deseret News*, February 17, 1943. INS's Honolulu main office was in the Young Hotel Building; RBJ took up residence at the Pacific Club, one of his favorite haunts.

108. Cable from Barry Faris, Editor-in-Chief, INS, New York to RBJ addressed to INS's Honolulu main office, dated January 28, 1942.

109. Letter, January 6, 1942, U. S. Pacific Fleet, U.S.S. *Pennsylvania,* Flagship, signed by Waldo Drake, Lt. Cmdr. USNR, Public Relations Officer.

110. See E.B. Potter, *Bull Halsey, A Biography* (Annapolis, MD: Naval Institute Press, 1985), pp. 15-17. See also Ralph B. Jordan, *Born to Fight* (Philadelphia: David McKay Co., 1946), pp. 126-127.

111. George W. Baer, *One Hundred Years of Sea Power: The U.S. Navy, 1890-1990* (Stanford, CA: Stanford University Press, 1994), p. 212.

112. Marc Milner, "Anglo-American Naval Co-operation in the Second World War, 1939-45," in John B. Hattendorf and Robert S. Jordan, eds. *Maritime Strategy and the Balance of Power: Britain and America in the Twentieth Century* (New York: St. Martin's Press, 1989), p. 258.

113. *San Francisco Call-Bulletin,* January 22, 1942, p. 1. RBJ recounted this episode in his book, *Born To Fight,* pp. 127-128.

114. Ralph Jordan, p. 128.

115. Baer, p. 212.

116. George C. Kenney, *General Kenney Reports: A Personal History of the Pacific War*, reprinted in the USAF Warrior Studies series, (Washington, D.C.: Office of Air Force History, 1987), p. 125.

117. *San Francisco Call-Bulletin*, March 10, 1942, p. 1. The headline was: "Yanks Flee Java, Says Reporter," and above the article was a map showing the invasion routes both taken and possibly contemplated by Japan.

118. William Manchester, *American Caesar: Douglas MacArthur, 1880-1914* (New York: Dell Publishing, 1978), p. 359.

119. *San Francisco Call-Bulletin*, April 8, 1942. See also Manchester, pp. 356ff). For a useful study of the treatment of the Japanese-Americans during World War II, see Page Smith, *Democracy on Trial* (New York: Simon and Schuster, 1995). RBJ's writings throughout this period were entirely reflective of the general attitude of the American public toward Japan and the Japanese or "Japs".

120. *San Francisco Call-Bulletin,* April 28, 1942.

121. For a good description of the Battle's various engagements, see Martin Stephen (as edited by Eric Grove), *Sea Battles in Closeup: World War 2* (Annapolis, MD: Naval Institute Press, 1991), pp. 137-158.

122. He also would have observed the action of the 19th Bomb Group, which at that time had B-17s (see Kenney, pp. 109ff). Later, based on Okinawa, his son Bob would be assigned to the Headquarters, 19th Bomb Group, when it was flying B-29s in the Korean War.

123. Gavin M. Long, as quoted in Manchester, pp. 344-345.

124. *Deseret News,* January 5, 1943.

125. *Deseret News*, January 6, 1943.

126. *Deseret News*, July 10, 1943.

127. *Deseret News*, July 10, 1943.

128. *Deseret News*, July 1, 1943.

129. *Deseret News*, July 8, 1943.

130. See Don Lohbeck, *Patrick J. Hurley* (Chicago: Henry Regnery Co., 1956), esp. pp. 158ff.

131. *San Francisco Call-Bulletin*, March 19, 1942.

132. *Deseret News*, August 14, 1943.

133. Desmond, p. 463.

134. Joseph J. Mathews, *Reporting the Wars* (Minneapolis: University of Minnesota Press, 1957), p. 195.

135. Letter, Captain H. D. Bode, Commanding Officer, USS *Chicago*, dated February 10, 1942.

136. *Deseret News*, August 5, 1943.

137. *Deseret News*, July 26, 1943.

138. Manchester, p. 354.

139. *Deseret News*, February 24, 1943.

140. *Deseret News*, February 12, 1943.

141. Wendell J. Ashton, *Voice in the West: Biography of a Pioneer Newspaper* (New York: Duell, Sloan and Pearce, 1950), p. 317.

142. The Church was not noted at the time for offering top salaries to its employees, whether executive rank or not. So it was noteworthy when, as was reported, Apostle Bowen talked about the "$10,000 a year editor" that the Church had hired (correspondence with Parry D. Sorensen, 17 October 1995).

143. INS Promotional Brochure, undated, although probably issued around 1934, when RBJ was with the Pacific Coast bureau of INS.

144. For more information, see Larry Stahle, *A Lasting Impression...A Press for All the World: A History of the Deseret Press, 1850-1980* (Salt Lake City: Deseret Press, 1980)). Their relationship also got off to a bad start when Petersen would not authorize RBJ to join the Alta Club, the pre-eminent business and professional club in the city. RBJ valued the club life for its own sake as well as for the business advantages it might bring, so this was especially annoying.

145. Correspondence with Wilby Durham, July 27, 1995.

146. For example, later, editorials were usually seen by Elder Gordon B. Hinckley, then a member of the Council of the Twelve and President of the Deseret News Publishing Company, and by President N. Eldon Tanner of the First Presidency (Swenson, p. 50).

147. An overview of how the Church is adapting to rapidly-changing times is given by Peter Steinfels, "Despite Growth, Mormons Find New Hurdles," *The New York Times*, September 15, 1991. One item discussed is the place of dissent among the Church membership. In a sense, this

issue is related to the question of what the appropriate role of Church-owned publications, including the newspaper, should be.

148. Correspondence with Wilby Durham, July 27, 1995.

149. During his tenure RBJ earned the respect of his chief colleagues, Wilby Durham (Circulation Manager), Theodore (Ted) Cannon (News Editor), and Theron Liddle (City Editor). They respected his journalistic professionalism. Howard Pearson covered movies and the press. Both Ted Cannon and Theron Liddle subsequently served as managing editors.

150. Paul Swenson, "Nostrums in the Newsroom: Raised Sights and Raised Expectations at the *Deseret News*," *Dialogue: A Journal of Mormon Thought*, Spring 1977, p. 50.

151. Swenson, p. 50.

152. Smart tried to develop the idea of a separate section of the *News* devoted to commentary on world events - similar to the *Church News* as a separate section. This seemed like an idea worth trying, as it would have brought the *Deseret News* closer to the model of *The Christian Science Monitor*, and that was RBJ's ideal. But nothing came of the idea. Interestingly, in the 1920s, before the special Church Section had been introduced, *The Improvement Era* had carried notations on world affairs. "Exploring the Universe" by Franklin S. Harris, and "These Times" by G. Homer Durham, were two such columns.

153. Decker has commented that his mother had camped on Smart's doorstep until he hired her son (correspondence with Parry Sorensen, 17 October 1995). Whatever the case, Smart was so impressed with him that Decker was made a twice-weekly critic at large in October 1974 (see Swenson, p. 49). Decker went on to become a Nieman Fellow at Harvard.

154. William Glaberson, "The Press: Bought and Sold and Gray All Over," *The New York Times*, July 30, 1945, p.E1. As for motion pictures, in 1995 the Disney conglomerate consisted of theme parks, fill and TV production, animation, film distribution, Capital Cities/ABC Inc., ABC television network, broadcast group, cable, publishing (including *Kansas City Star* an *Fort Worth Star-Telegram*), etc. (Geraldine Fabrikant, "Walt Disney Acquiring ABC in Deal Worth $19

Billion; Entertainment Giant Born," *The New York Times*, August 1, 1995, p.1)

155. A lively description, partly culled from the files of the *Deseret News*, of how Utah celebrated the first centennial of the American Union, is found in Richard Poll, "The Americanization of Utah," *Utah Historical Quarterly*, Winter, 1976, pp. 76-93. As Poll put it: "I will argue that even when Utah was most different, she was in most respects not so very different. I will suggest that any disposition to emphasize differences has long since given way to a desire to be the most American of all." (p. 78).

156. Ashton, pp. 320-321. Earlier, there had been an INS linkage with the *News*: "The encouragement of radio in the mountains by the *Deseret News* took a big step on November 20, 1920, when the newspaper announced that on the following Monday evening (November 22) it would begin nightly wireless news flashes. They were to be *Deseret News*-International News Service bulletins." (Ashton, p. 269)

157. It was reported that Pusey wanted $500 a month, and that the Church considered this too high a salary (correspondence with Parry Sorensen, October 17, 1995). Pusey later won the Pulitzer Prize and the Bancroft Prize for his two-volume biography of Justice Charles Evans Hughes. He also wrote *Builders of the Kingdom*, published by Brigham Young University Press in 1981. Interestingly, RBJ and Pusey might have ended up working for the same person because in the late 1920s , when there were attempts by William Randolph Hearst to buy the *Washington Post* (Merlo J. Pusey, "My Fifty Years in Journalism," *Dialogue: A Journal of Mormon Thought*, Spring, 1977, pp. 70-81). Leslie G. Midgley, a former city editor of the *News* who later was with the *New York Herald-Tribune*, also had Utah journalistic connections.

158. Cited in Frank W. Fox, *J. Reuben Clark: The Public Years* (Provo, UT: Brigham Young University Press/Deseret Book Company, 1980), p. 438-439.

159. The afternoon paper in Washington, the *Washington Times*, is owned by the Reverend Sun Myung Moon's Unification Church.

160. Taken from the essay by Professor William E. Turcotte, *et. al.,* "Innovation and Change," written for the National

Security Decision Making Department, United States Naval War College, Newport, R.I. undated, p. 4. As revealed earlier, RBJ also was the "outsider" when working for Aimee Semple McPherson because he was not a member of her Four-Square church and had no interest in the ecclesiastical side of her ministry.

161. Correspondence with Wilby Durham, July 27, 1995.

162. *Deseret News*, January 7, 1943. This is but one of countless examples that RBJ could "spin a yarn" with the best of them!

163. See Ashton.

164. See Cowan. See also J. Cecil Alter, *Early Utah Journalism: A Half Century of Forensic Warfare, Waged by the West's Most Militant Press* (Westport, CN: Greenwood Press, Publishers, 1970 - first published in 1938 by the Utah State Historical Society).

165. Today this is the trend in urban/suburban publishing, sometimes through introducing specially-tailored editions for the various suburbs rather than linking-up with an existing suburban paper.

166. There also was not, at this time, a Sunday edition to compete with the *Sunday Tribune*. There were four daily editions: the "Noon" which covered street sales and Idaho towns; the "Two-star" which covered both northern Utah to Logan and southern Utah to St. George and Mesquite and Las Vegas, Nevada; the "Home" edition covering Salt Lake, Provo to Ogden; and the "Pink" handling street sales and mail copies outside the circulation area (correspondence with Wilby Durham, July 27, 1995).

167. O.N. Malmquist, *The First Hundred Years: A History of the Salt Lake Tribune, 1871-1971* (Salt Lake City: Utah State Historical Society, 1971), p. 36.

168. Malmquist, p. 372; see also Ashton, Ch. XII.

169. RBJ likely was influenced by Hearst's belief in the value of cartoons to stimulate reader interest (see St. Johns, p. 126).

170. *Deseret News*, June 26, 1943. Two books which chronicle some of the dispatches of the correspondents featured in the *Deseret News* by RBJ were: *Reporting World War II,* Vols. I, II (New York: The Library of America, 1995); Jack Stenbuck,

ed., *Typewriter Battalion: Dramatic Front-Line Dispatches* (New York: William Morrow and Co., 1995).

171. The column became so popular that not long afterward the *Tribune* started a local column written by O.M. Malmquist (correspondence with Wilby Durham, July 27, 1995). When RBJ found it inconvenient to write a column, he printed some of the stories by Ernie Pyle when Pyle was covering the war in North Africa.

172. *Deseret News*, December 31, 1942. Another "outsider" Mormon convert was hired in 1947 to write a column to discuss world affairs; Vivian Meik, an Englishman, wrote "Vivian Meik Says" (see Ashton, pp. 324-325).

173. *Deseret News*, July 14, 1943. The "queen" was Miss Pat Pixton, whose father, Col. Robert C. Pixton, was with RBJ in Honolulu just after Pearl Harbor.

174. *Deseret News*, February 24, 1943.

175. *Deseret News*, February 2, 1943.

176. For background, see Ralph V. Chamberlin, *The University of Utah: A History of Its First Hundred Years, 1850 to 1950* (Salt Lake City: University of Utah Press, 1960). For background on President Cowles, see LeRoy E. Cowles, *University of Utah and World War II* (Salt Lake City: The Deseret News Press, 1949).

177. *Deseret News*, August 8, 1943. Gregg said that Utah was being "quietly drained of talent." A year later - the Jordans and the Greggs would find themselves living in the same community in New York.

178. *Deseret News*, March 23, 1944. See also Dennis L. Lythgoe, "A Special Relationship: J. Bracken Lee and the Mormon Church," *Dialogue: A Journal of Mormon History,* Winter, 1978.

179. *Deseret News*, August 11, 1943. Jenkins was a famous race car driver before entering politics.

180. *Deseret News*, August 4, 1943. He compared favorably Maw's charm as a public speaker to Roosevelt's. John Gunther agreed with RBJ: "[Maw] is a former professor of oratory and one of the best public speakers in the United States" (quoted in Herbert B. Maw, *Adventures With Life* (Salt Lake City, UT: Privately published, 1978), p. 128).

181. See *Deseret News*, August 9, 1943, and August 23, 1943.

182. Ashton, p. 322. Referring to the chaotic times, Ashton declared dramatically: "For the people in the mountaintops, it was a beacon in the storm" (p. 323).

183. Harry Hansen, *Scarsdale: From Colonial Manor to Modern Community* (New York: Harper and Brothers, 1954), p. 6.

184. According to Mary, RBJ was being groomed by Joseph Connolly of INS's parent company, King Features Syndicate, to replace Faris, who had been the editor-in-chief since 1916. Faris had made his mark as the newsman who "broke" the Lindbergh baby kidnaping case (see, for example, references to Faris in Clay Blair, *The Forgotten War: America in Korea, 1950-1953* (New York: Doubleday, 1987), p. 524; and William Manchester, *American Caesar: Douglas MacArthur, 1880-1914* (New York: Dell Publishing, 1978), p. 733).

185. Carol O'Connor, *A Sort of Utopia: Scarsdale, 1891-1981* (Albany: State University of New York Press, 1983), pp. 7-8.

186. Hansen, pp. 3-4.

187. See O'Connor, Ch. 5.

188. O'Connor, p. 66.

189. O'Connor, p. 172. O'Connor also mentions a successor, Harold Howe II, who became U.S. Commissioner of Education and a Vice President of the Ford Foundation.

190. The *Maroon*, December 20, 1944. Mary Ellen was the News Editor that year.

191. Letter of October 6, 1945. The counselors in the branch presidency at the time were Arthur H. Neeley and Stanley McAllister. Mary was Relief Society secretary.

192. Clarence Streit, *Union Now With Britain* (New York: Harper and Bros., 1941).

193. Wofford later held high positions in the Kennedy Administration, and was a Senator from Pennsylvania briefly just before and during the Clinton Administration. After losing his bid for re-election, Wofford became head of the Clinton Administration's domestic volunteer Americorps program, modeled after the Peace Corps. Harris Wofford's younger brother, Jack, was a Rhodes Scholar at Oxford University at the same time that Bob was studying at St. Antony's College for his doctorate.

194. See Cord Meyer, *Facing Reality: From World Federalism to the CIA* ((New York: Harper and Row, 1980).

195. The United World Federalists movement still exists, and there is a World Association of World Federalists (see George A. Codding, "World federalism: the conceptual setting," in A.J.R. Groom and P. Taylor, eds. *Frameworks for International Cooperation* (London: Pinter Publishers, 1990), pp. 217-233.

196. He was President of the Board in 1950-51.

197. O'Connor cited a *New York Times Magazine* article of April 1969 about Scarsdale, and she compared Scarsdale and Logan. She joined the History Department of Utah State University when her book was published (see pp. 214 and 221).

198. Another Mormon diasporan, Mark Cannon discusses some of these same points in regard to Short Hills, New Jersey, where he lived in the late 1960s while serving as President of the Institute of Public Administration in New York (see Mark W. Cannon, "Mormons in the Executive Suite," *Dialogue: A Journal of Mormon Thought*, Autumn, 1968, pp. 97-108).

199. 199Letter from Barry Faris to Lee Van Atta, December, 1944.

200. The family seldom went into New York City, although a memorable night was going to Times Square to celebrate the victory over Germany....it was packed and the air was electric with excitement.

201. During the summer of 1945, Mary Ellen also worked there, and the twins became greens-men at the Scarsdale Golf Club, which gave them club privileges. The club was located in Hartsdale, not far from Greenacres. Some of the boys who also had summer jobs there lived near Bob and Bill, but they attended prep schools during the academic year.

202. Unfortunately, RBJ's father died unexpectedly in California during RBJ's hospitalization, so he was unable to attend his father's funeral. The final arrangements were left to Burdette, who was still stationed in California with the Navy. In the 1970s, Bob had minor surgery in the White Plains Hospital, as did his daughter, Mary Rebecca "Becky" - a reminder that there is more than one way for generational paths to cross!

203. Letter from the General Headquarters, Southwest Pacific Area, dated March 15, 1945.

204. Ralph B. Jordan, *Born To Fight* (Philadelphia: David McKay Co., 1946). Bob dedicated a book to RBJ on naval affairs that he co-edited with Professor John B. Hattendorf of the Naval War College to RBJ: *Maritime Strategy and the Balance of Power: Britain and America in the Twentieth Century* (London: Macmillan Press, and New York: St. Martin's Press, 1989). He also co-dedicated a book to both of his parents: Thomas G. Weiss and Robert S. Jordan, *The World Food Conference and Global Problem Solving* (New York: Praeger Publishers, 1976).

205. See, for example, Thomas J. Cutler, *The Battle of Leyte Gulf: 23-26 October 1944* (New York: HarperCollins Publishers, 1994), and E.B. Potter, *Bull Halsey* (Annapolis, MD: Naval Institute Press, 1985). Potter commented on RBJ's book "I use Jordan with caution. His book is undocumented and contains obvious errors, but he interviewed Admiral Halsey's wife and mother and possibly the admiral himself" (p. 394). In fairness, RBJ was asked by a commercial publisher to write a popular, largely impressionistic book about the admiral at the height of the national acclaim over Halsey's wartime exploits, not a historical treatise.

206. Other titles being promoted by David McKay Company at this time (no connection to the Mormon Church leader of the same name), were Captain W. P. McCahill, *First to Fight, The United States Marines*; Captain William Crawford, Jr., as told to Ted Saucier, *Gore and Glory*; Rutherford Montgomery, *Rough Riders Ho!*; and Rutherford Montgomery, *Sea Raiders Ho!*.

207. R.S. Jordan, p. 206.

208. Ralph Jordan, pp. 163-164. He also drew upon his file of wartime dispatches during his first tour of duty in the Southwest Pacific.

209. Paul Fussell, *Wartime: Understanding and Behavior in the Second World War* (New York: Oxford University Press, 1989), p. 59. Unfortunately, Fred's naval career as a medical corpsman did not engender the same parental feelings of pride.

210. According to his oral history, Admiral Royer - including when he was commanding the Oakland Supply Center - perceived the importance of good community and public relations. So he naturally gravitated toward those newspapermen who would help him to accomplish this - RBJ, obviously, being one with whom he had developed a more lasting tie (see his oral history, dated July 12, 1972, at the Naval Institute Oral History collection, Annapolis, Maryland).

211. O'Connor, p. 153.

212. Quoted in Erikson, p. 29.

213. Mary Ellen worked one summer in MGM's fan mail department, thus coming to appreciate the importance of that public relations function. On the place of fan mail in the industry, see Rosten, Appendix H.

214. Jonathan Snow, as recounted in RBJ's "Newsman's Notes" column, *Deseret News*, August 26, 1943.

215. Leonard Quart and Albert Auster, *American Film and Society Since 1945*, 2nd ed., (New York: Praeger, 1991), p. 17.

216. Taken from Richard Griffith and Arthur Mayer, *The Movies: The Sixty-Year Story of the World of Hollywood and Its Effect on America, from the Pre-Nickelodeon Days to the Present* (New York: Simon and Schuster, 1957).

217. Griffith and Mayer.

218. The writer-director Abraham Polonsky, quoted in Quart and Auster, p. 21.

219. Eames, pp. 9 and 8 respectively.

220. Stephanie Walton, "1952 Olympians honor coach, goalie," *El Segundo Herald*, undated. The same team represented the United States in the first Pan American Games in 1951. See also Jim and Lynne Norris, *Uhro Saari, Olympian* (Los Olivos, CA: Olive Grove Publications, 1988).

221. The renaissance shortly later suffered a setback when one of the main approaches to the new Los Angeles Airport was carved out of the middle of the community. The Westport Beach Club no longer exists, probably a casualty of road expansion along the beach.

222. *Deseret News*, February 19, 1943.

223. When they lived on Van Ness Avenue, Mary and RBJ would go to the races at Rancho Santa Anita on his press pass.

224. RBJ was never sent to a hospital for tests, nor was he examined by a specialist, or entered into any kind of a rehabilitation program.
225. Letter, September 10, 1951.
226. The Sigma Chi chapters at Utah State and the University of Utah were very strong, and from them came many young men who went on to distinguished careers.
227. Richard L. Evans, *The Everlasting Things* (New York: Harper and Bros., 1957); also *Unto the Hills* (New York: Harper and Bros., 1940).
228. *Unto the Hills*, p. 7.
229. For more on Bob and both his own and his family's lives, see Robert Smith Jordan, *A Diasporan Mormon's Life: Essays of Remembrance* (New York: iUniverse, 2009).
230. Bob also received the United Nations Service Medal and the Korean Service Medal.
231. It turned out that General Hutchinson was also a Sigma Chi, so the base public affairs office sent a story, with photograph, to *The Magazine of Sigma Chi,* which used it in the issue of October 1953.
232. RBJ would have taken pride in the dedication of the Korean War memorial in Washington, D.C. in July 1995; as his writings, especially the recollections contained in his "Newsman's Notes," RBJ took every opportunity to honor those Americans who fought for their "flag and country" (See Peter Grier, "US Remembers Its 'Forgotten War,' *The Christian Science Monitor,* July 26, 1995, p. 1).
233. Everyone was there except Bill; Mary advised him not to return from Philadelphia, where he was in the midst of examinations at Temple University Medical School.
234. Interview with Jane Jordan, October 26, 1995.
235. Interview with Jane Jordan, October 26, 1995.
236. Evans, *Unto The Hills,* p.18.
237. For a very good examination of success-oriented Mormon business executives, see Mark W. Cannon, "Mormons in the Executive Suite," *Dialogue: A Journal of Mormon Thought,* Autumn, 1968, pp. 96-108. Cannon mentioned the Lochinvar Club, a club composed of high-level business and corporate executives of Utah origins in the New York City area. If the Lochinvar Club had existed in his time in

New York City, RBJ doubtless would have been a member. Two of his contemporaries, and neighbors in Scarsdale, were listed as members in 1968 - G. Stanley McAllister and Isaac M. Stewart. Mary's half-cousin, Morris B. Wright of Kuhn and Loeb investment bankers, was also listed. Another of their lifelong friends, O. Leslie Stone, has a short career biography in the article.

238. Cannon, p. 105.

239. See Charles M. Hatch, *Creating Ethnicity in the Hydraulic Village of the Mormon West*, an unpublished masters thesis, Utah State University, 1991. Hatch claims that the second or third generations of the very large families of the pioneers, had to look elsewhere for their livelihoods because of the shortage of land and water. He also observes that the loss of eligible males created pressures on marriageable women, which might explain why Mary did not want to be left behind when RBJ decided to go to California!

240. For biographical sketches of these men who went on to California, see Leo J. Muir, *A Century of Mormon Activities in California,* vols. 1 and 2 (Salt Lake City: Deseret News Press, 1952). Another source is Julian C. Lowe and Florian H. Thayn, eds., *History of the Mormons in the Greater Washington Area: Members of the Church of Jesus Christ of Latter-Day Saints in the Washington D.C. Area, 1839-1991* (Washington, D.C.: Community Printing Service, Inc., 1991)).

241. Kimball taught economics at the University of Utah before going into investment banking in Chicago. For his obituary, see *The American Oxonian,* Winter, 1995, pp. 107-108.

242. Such pressures did not always shape in a felicitous way the lives of the children of these achievement-oriented Mormon parents. In nearly every one of the families mentioned by Mark Cannon, there has been one or more children for whom the strain of attempting to meet consistently high - and in some cases unattainable - parental expectations resulted in emotional disturbances that profoundly affected their lives.

243. Fox, p. 603.

244. Jan Shipps, "In the Presence of the past: Continuity and Change in Twentieth Century Mormonism" in Thomas G. Alexander and Jessie L. Embry, eds., *After 150, The Latter-*

day Saints in Sesquicentennial Perspective (Provo, UT: The Charles Redd Center for Western Studies, 1983), p. 14.

245. The widows of Utahns who made their careers elsewhere often would return to Utah after their husbands' deaths. For example, the Cannon sisters - Adele Cannon Howells (Mrs. David P.), Jeanne Cannon Hunter (Mrs. William E.), and Marion Cannon Bennion (Mrs. Howard S.) returned "home" after their very professionally prominent husbands in either Los Angeles or New York died.

246. David Riesman, *The Lonely Crowd: A Study of the Changing American Character*, (New Haven: Yale University Press, 1961), p.149.

247. Gordon Shepherd and Gary Shepherd, *A Kingdom Transformed: Themes in the Development of Mormonism* (Salt Lake City: University of Utah Press, 1984), pp. 173-174.

248. One seemingly minor example is that the official Church logo has been changed to emphasis "Jesus Christ" rather than "Latter-day-Saints." Overall, the church is linked more closely to conservative than to liberal Protestantism, although retaining its sectarian doctrines of exclusivity.

249. Fox, p. 439.

250. Mary Ellen died in 2009, and Bob survives. Fred died in 1981 after suffering for years with lymphatic cancer. He is buried in the Hillcrest Cemetery in Redlands, California, not far from Mary and RBJ. Burdette died in 1989 of heart disease, and is buried in Bakersfield, California. Bill died in 1992 from various causes, some reaching back to his boyhood illnesses when his heart and lungs were weakened due to asthma and allergies. He is buried in Heber, Utah.

251. Statement by Brigham Young in 1848, quoted by Ray Allen Billington, *Westward Expansion: A History of the American Frontier*, 3rd. ed. (New York: The Macmillan Co., 1967), p. 542.

252. The lineage traced here for RBJ is his mother's. The Jordan lineage has been more difficult to identify. Mary's Mormon lineage is better known because her grandparents came from the British Isles and migrated much later to America, and because there have been many Mormon descendants who hired researchers to scour the records in England and here.

253. This information, and much more concerning the origins of the Hangers, is derived from the unpublished genealogical monograph of Peggy S. Joyner, comp., "Frederich and Peter Hanger of Virginia, 1740 Immigrants: Some Ancestors and Descendants," dated March 1977, and revised October 1986. A copy of the monograph is at the Family History Library of The Church of Jesus Christ of Latter-day Saints in Salt Lake City, Utah.

254. Dan Elbert Clark, *The West in American History* (New York: Thomas Y. Crowell Co., 1937), p. 85.

255. Elizabeth A. Kessel, "Germans in the Making of Frederick Country, Maryland," in Robert D. Mitchell, ed., *Appalachian Frontiers: Settlement, Society and Development in the Preindustrial Era* (Lexington, KY: The University of Kentucky Press, 1991), p. 92.

256. C. E. Kemper, quoted by Clark, p. 89.

257. See, for example, Mitchell.

258. Joyner, p. 2.

259. Mitchell, pp. 95-96.

260. *The Handy Book for Genealogists*, 8th ed. (Logan, UT: The Everton Publishers, 1991), p. M-49.

261. Billington, p. 247. Some of the Hangers themselves owned plantations in Virginia around Staunton, and had one or more slaves (see Joyner).

262. Interestingly, an early settler named the Champaign county seat "Urbana" in 1802, after the Urbana in Greenbrier County, Virginia, from whence he had migrated (Charles S. Wood, "Sketches of the Early History of Champaign County, Ohio," *Champaign Democrat*, June 15, 1905).

263. Extract from special centennial edition of a local newspaper, 1878, photocopied from the Logan County Public Library collection by Robert S. Jordan, April 11, 1994.

264. Thomas added the "X" for the same reason that President Harry Truman had the "S" in his name - to distinguish himself from all the other Smiths named Thomas when he left his home in England to come to America.

265. It took an average of thirty-eight days to cross from Liverpool to New Orleans; the average size of a ship's immigrant company was 271. (See William G. Hartley's review of Conway B. Sonne, *Saints on the Seas: A Maritime History of*

Mormon Migration, 1830-1890 (Salt Lake City: University of Utah Press, 1983), in *Brigham Young University Studies*, Spring 1985, p. 87); also Susan Arrington Madsen, *I Walked to Zion: True Stories of Young Pioneers on the Mormon Trail* (Salt Lake City: Deseret Book Co., 1994).

266. See Thomas X. Smith's history. Also to be noted is the work of David Barkdull - a descendant of Thomas X. Smith through his second wife, Anne Masters Howe - who has compiled a summary of the various memoirs of Thomas X. Smith's children, adding some new information of his own. For a history of this migration along the "Mormon Trail," see W.J. Ghent, *The Road to Oregon: A Chronicle of the Great Emigrant Trail* (New York: Longmans, Green and Co., 1929), esp. Ch. V.

267. William Edwin Berrett, *The Restored Church*, 16th ed. (Salt Lake City: Deseret Book Co., 1974), pp. 286-287. A chronicle that parallels the Smiths' migration, although landing at New York rather than New Orleans is "A Diary kept by Caroline Hopkins Clark on Journey from England to the Valley in the Mountains, April 30, 1866 to September 23, 1866, and Letters to England." This is on file with the LDS Church Family History Library.

268. See Julie A. Dockstader, "Little-known pioneers remembered," *Church News*, Week Ending July 27, 1991, p. 14. The Mormon settlers first came into Cache Valley in 1856 under the leadership of Peter Maughan, but there had been many trappers and traders - "mountain men" - who had passed through the valley from 1810 to 1840. Maughan's party originated in the Toole area. Wright's group of twenty families were gathered from as far south as Draper and as far north as Farmington.

269. *Cache Valley: In and Out and 'Round About*, a monograph prepared by Yvonne Young Merrill with the partial support of the Utah State University Faculty Women's League, 1970, p. 8. Merrill reports that in 1860 there were thirty-nine polygamists in the valley, seven percent of the population (p.11).

270. "Pioneer Edition of Events in the Early History of Logan and Cache Valley," p. 3 - a pamphlet prepared by Al. J. Curtis, 1946, in the LDS Family History Library. Mary Ellen Smith

put the date of the appointment of the committee as May 6, 1858. She also reported : "On May 9 they began to break the land and plant wheat, vegetables and water melons. John P. Wright held the plow that plowed the first furrow." (See Mary E. Smith, "Interesting Sketch of Logan by the Relief Society... ." (n.p., n.d.), in Morgan G. Evans, *Financial Papers and Sketches*, Logan, Cache County, Utah, 1852-1900, on file in LDS Church Family History Library).

271. Dockstader. See also Andrew Jensen, *Latter-day Saints Biographical Encyclopedia*, vol. 1.

272. Thomas X. Smith's history. Orson Smith's first wife, Carolyn Carpenter, named the town.

273. The original log cabin built by John F. Wright at what is now Sagamore Farm still exists. Later, a New England-style white frame farmhouse was built. The landscaping included a formal, aspen-lined circular drive added by Orville Lee (husband of Martha Wright Smith Lee), and gave the farm a certain distinction. Unfortunately, the house burned down; years later the huge dairy barn also burned. Many family memories spanning five generations were thus lost. The farm still remains in the Lee family. For life on Sagamore Farm, see Christian C. Lee, "One Day in the Life of Chris Lee on Sagamore Farm," undated.

274. Life of Mary Ellen Wright Smith, by Martha Smith Lee, undated.

275. See "My History" by Olena Wright Smith Harris for a detailed description of Grandpa Smith's Logan properties in and around Logan.

276. See Orson Smith's history; also Ricks.

277. Interview with Mrs. Watson, p. 4. He also had asked a fourth girl but was refused, the girl preferring to marry into monogamy.

278. Watson.

279. Mary Ellen Smith also qualified to teach, but, as she said: "[I] went to the B.Y. to school for a year after Nellie was born [April 27, 1885]. My mother took care of Nellie. I didn't graduate but they gave me a certificate to teach. I was pregnant with Martha and couldn't graduate as I had to go away" (Mary Ellen Wright Smith's history). This meant going into hiding or away from Utah.

280. According to Mrs. Margaret Carpenter Smith Watson, the term "week about" was used to mean one week at a time with each wife (interview March 25, 1937).

281. Mary Ellen Wright's history, undated. Martha Lee's version states that Mary Ellen Smith attended school in Draper for one year because the Draper schools were better than those in Logan. Stewart was highly regarded in the community, as this tribute shows: "Dr. George Thomas, once a pupil at the Brigham Young College, speaks in reminiscence of his old teacher's kindliness, human sympathy, and personal interest in those under his tuition. His theological classes seemed to have an especial appeal." (Marian Stewart, "The Story of J.Z. Stewart," typescript, Logan, 1934, p. 9) Stewart later served on the Logan Stake High Council when Orson Smith was the Stake President. (See Curtis, p. 18) Thomas became president of the college.

282. See Mary Ellen Wright Smith's history.

283. Mary Ellen Wright Smith's history.

284. Letter to Robert S. Jordan, June 2, 1958.

285. William Jordan's history of Mary Wright Smith, delivered as a eulogy at her funeral on December 31, 1980.

286. William Jordan.

287. That the Church looked the other way at this continued cohabitation is evidenced by the fact: "The eleven General Authorities guilty of unlawful cohabitation in the years 1890-1905 had a total of twenty-seven wives bearing children and seventy-six children." (Kenneth L. Cannon III, "Beyond the manifesto: Polygamous Cohabitation among LDS General Authorities after 1890," *Utah Historical Quarterly*, Winter 1978, p. 31). Incidentally, divorce was more prevalent among polygamists than is generally acknowledged. (See Eugene E. Campbell and Bruce L. Campbell, "Divorce among Mormon Polygamists: Extent and Explanations," *Utah Historical Quarterly*, Winter, 1978, pp. 5-23).

288. See Gustave D. Larsen, *The Americanization of Utah for Statehood* (San Marino, CA: The Huntington Library, 1971). President Joseph F. Smith had admitted in testimony in 1904 in connection with the investigation of Senator Smoot that he had: "...continued cohabitation with his plural wives, of whom he had five. He stated that since 1890, the date of

the Woodruff Manifesto outlawing polygamy, he had been the Father of eleven children, and that each of his wives had been the mother of at least one of them." (Quoted in Gordon C. Thomason, "The Manifesto was a Victory!" *Dialogue: A Journal of Mormon Thought*, spring 1971, p. 45).

289. The Stake-level structure was weaker in those days than it is today. The Bishop was involved in the temporal as well as the spiritual affairs of his members (see Ricks).

290. Billington, p.548. This practice began under the provisions of the State of Deseret (1849).

291. Interview with Mrs. Watson, June 10, 1938, p. 1.

292. It was fairly common among men of Orson Smith's generation to write poetry, just as it was to keep a journal or diary.

Index

Y